Julia Edkins

IRISH FAMINE FACTS

JOHN KEATING

Teagasc

Agriculture and Food Development Authority

Acknowledgements

This publication had its origins in a major exhibition organised by Teagasc (The Agriculture and Food Development Authority) and the Department of Agriculture, Food and Forestry to commemorate the 150th Anniversary of the Irish Famine. In preparing for the exhibition, the focus was on presenting the central facts in a concise format. That format has been retained in this publication.

In researching the story of the Famine, the great body of scholarly work now published on the period was explored. In particular, extensive use was made of the great wealth of information contained in the published works of Austin Bourke, Cormac O'Grada, Mary Daly and Cecil Woodham-Smith. A full bibliography of the works consulted is listed.

The illustrations and photographs included are an important element of the publication. In this regard I wish to pay particular thanks to the staff of the National Library of Ireland, to Charles Godson, Teagasc and to the library staff, Department of Agriculture, Food and Forestry.

The Famine Commemorative Exhibition could not have been researched and compiled without the support and help of the organising committee: John Burke, Pat Comerford, Liam Downey, Leslie Dowley, Ronan Gormley, Harry Kehoe, Tom Maher and Austin OíSullivan, Teagasc and Pat Duffy, Dick Kennelly, Vincent McCarthy and Kevin O'Donoghue, Department of Agriculture, Food and Forestry. The support of Minister Ivan Yates TD also greatly facilitated the effort involved.

I would also like to acknowledge the help of Tom Maher for his comments during the draft stages. Crucial support was also provided by my wife Mary, colleagues Amelia Davin, Colette Gallagher and Dr Liam Downey, Director, Teagasc.

This book is published to accompany the videotape, also entitled Famine Facts.

Published by **Teagasc**,
19 Sandymount Avenue, Ballsbridge, Dublin 4, Ireland

First published, June 1996

ISBN 0-901317-46-2

Design by DBA Publications
Printed in Ireland by The Kilkenny People

Contents

	Foreword	***4***
1.	***Background to the Famine***	***5***
2.	***The Potato in Ireland***	***23***
3.	***Blight***	***29***
4.	***Government Relief Schemes***	***35***
5.	***The Famine 1845-1849***	***45***
6.	***Private and Workhouse Relief Efforts***	***55***
7.	***Consequences of the Famine***	***63***
8.	***The Search for a Cure***	***77***
	Lessons from the Famine Experience	***84***
	Bibliography	*86*
	List of illustrations	*87*

Foreword

The Famine, which affected Ireland between 1845 and 1850, is the most tragic event in Irish history. In the five years of the Famine, it is estimated that at least one million men, women and children died and a further one million emigrated. The scale of the disaster is aptly summarised in a quotation cited by the historian Cormac O'Gráda: *"Almost a quarter of the population emigrated to either the New World or the Next World in a period of little more than five years"*.

The Famine was triggered by the fungal disease blight, which first struck the potato crop in the Autumn of 1845. It struck again in 1846, totally destroying the potato crop on which so many people depended for food. The consequences were devastating.

Images of famine now seen on television from other parts of the world - hunger, disease, fever, emaciated bodies, death and mass graves were common throughout Ireland. Men, women and children died in their homes, on relief works, on the road seeking relief, in the streets of towns where they sought help, in the workhouses and in the countryside. Some were buried in mass graves, others were left where they lay and their houses tumbled on them.

Controversy still continues over whether more could have been done to help the people. At the time, Ireland was an integral part of the United Kingdom, then the wealthiest and the most powerful country in the world. Consequently many argue that Ireland did not get the help it was due in a time of need. No doubt, distrust of the rebellious Catholic Irish and the harsh economic philosophies of the time influenced Government actions.

Attitudes and events set in train by the Famine have played a major role in shaping modern Ireland. Emigration, particularly to America, continued. The landlord to tenant leasing system then in operation was decried. Demands for land ownership and self government soon became the order of the day. The outcome is todays Ireland.

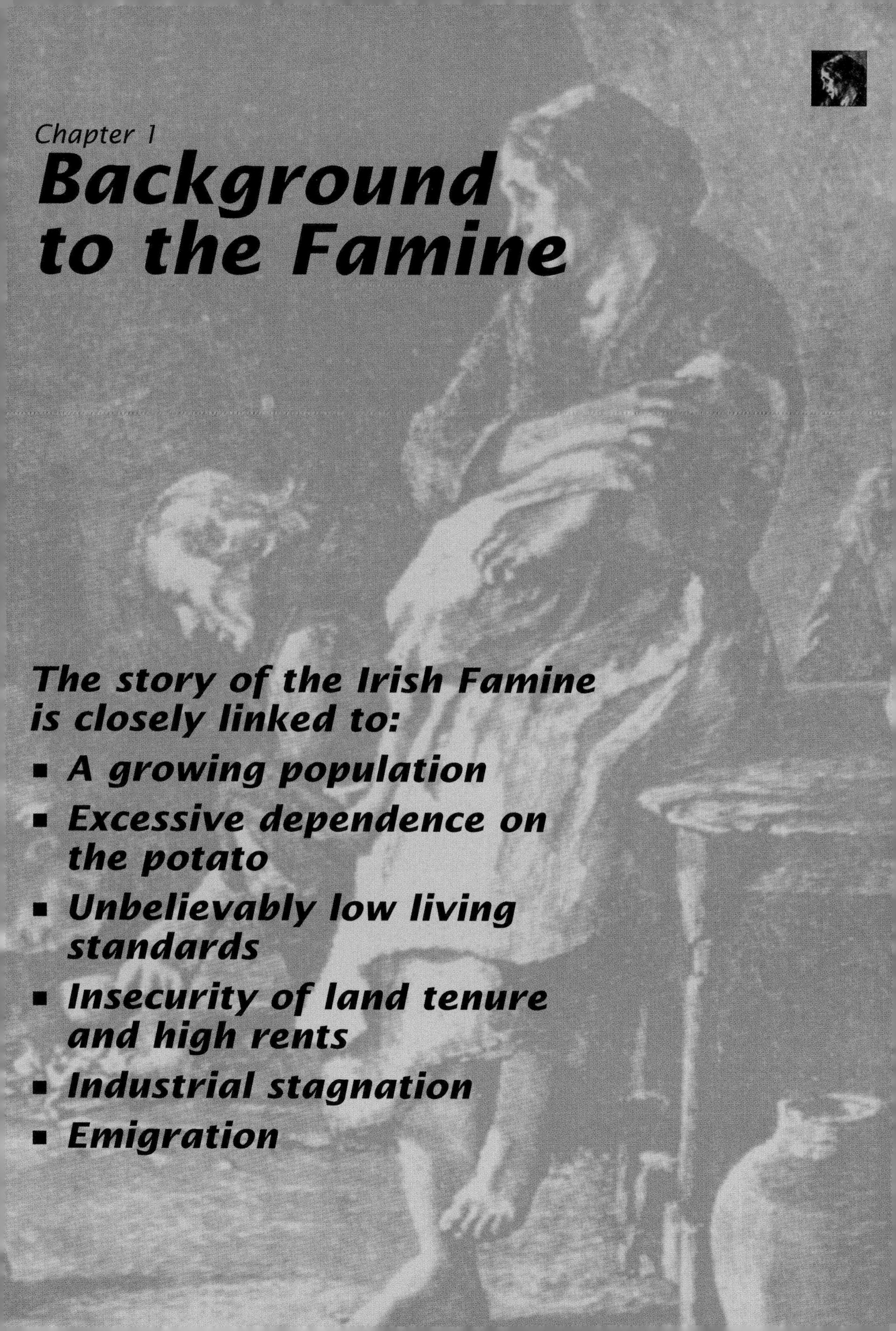

Chapter 1

Background to the Famine

The story of the Irish Famine is closely linked to:

- ***A growing population***
- ***Excessive dependence on the potato***
- ***Unbelievably low living standards***
- ***Insecurity of land tenure and high rents***
- ***Industrial stagnation***
- ***Emigration***

Background to the Famine

A Growing Population

Following the wars and plantations of the sixteenth and seventeenth centuries, the population of Ireland began to rise. By 1754 it had reached 2.4 million. In the following ninety years the population increased from 2.4 to 8.2 million (Figure 1). The potato played an important role in supporting this rapid growth in population.

Figure 1: Irish population 1695 - 1841

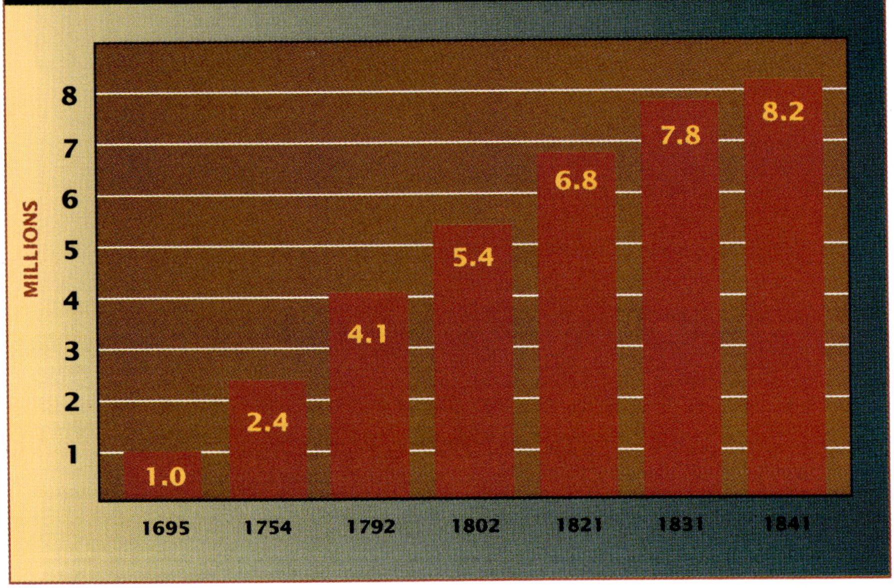

Reasons

Among the reasons put forward for the unprecedented growth in population after 1750 are:

- The prosperity of industry and agriculture between 1750 and 1815 - the removal of trade sanctions (1778/79), the industrial revolution, the American War of Independence (1775-1783) and the Napoleonic Wars (1793 - 1815), all contributed to this prosperity.
- The Corn Laws (1815) which restricted the importation of American and Canadian grain and created a protected market for corn in Britain. This led to a high demand for agricultural labour.

- More stable food supply - the change from a dairy based diet to a cereal and potato diet guaranteed more food from the existing land area.
- High marriage rate - 90% of the population were marrying. The sub-division of holdings made early marriages possible.
- Early marriages - generally about 22 years for women and 23 years for men.
- Large families - children were a security for parents in old age since there was no social welfare system in existence.
- Better health - improved hygiene and vaccination reduced deaths from epidemics and smallpox.

Dependence on the Potato

The rise in population was accompanied by an increase in the amount of potatoes grown. The area sown increased from about 180,000 hectares in 1725 to 860,000 hectares in 1845 (Figure 2). As the area sown increased, more of the potato crop was grown on poor land.

Figure 2: Area of potatoes grown 1695 - 1841

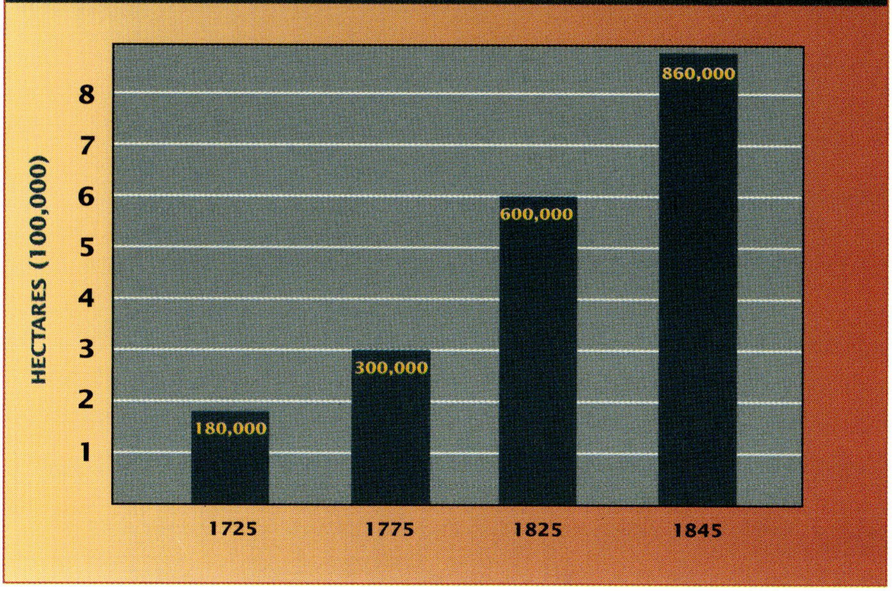

After Bourke, Davidson and Salaman.

In total, approximately 15 million tonnes of potatoes were consumed annually in Ireland in the early 1840's. Seven million tonnes were used for human food and 5 million tonnes for animal feed mainly to pigs, poultry, cattle and horses. A further two million tonnes were used for seed while a small quantity was exported. Some would also have rotted or decayed in the storage pits. The pre-famine use of potatoes is summarised in Figure 3.

Figure 3: Pre-Famine use of potatoes

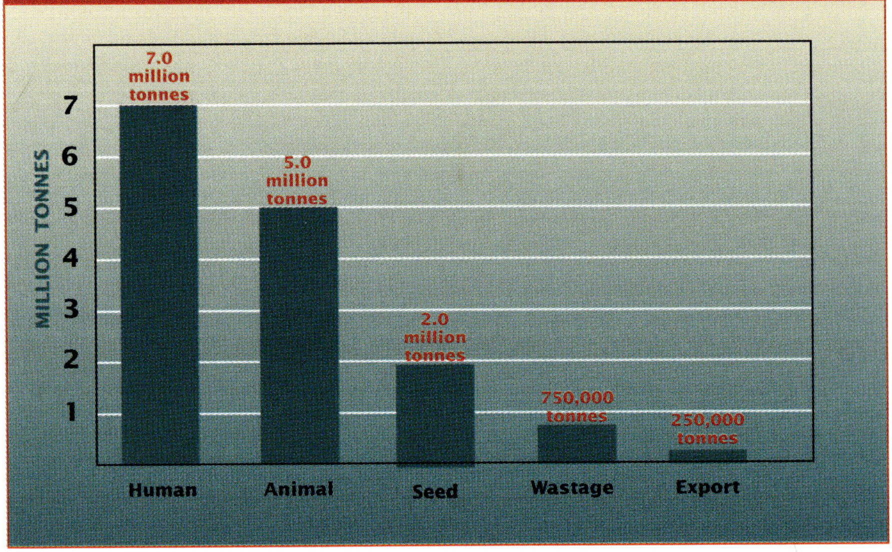

After Bourke, Davidson and Salaman.

Potatoes in the Diet

In pre-famine Ireland, labourers, cottiers, smallholders and their families depended almost exclusively on the potato as a source of food. Individuals consumed enormous quantities by today's standards (Table 1). The poor, however, were not alone in making extensive use of the potato in their diet. This is aptly summarised in the following quotation from Salaman.

> *"If necessity made the potato the food of the masses, the habit it created was certainly not confined to them. The middle class, though free to choose a more varied diet became confirmed potato addicts and consumed what we today would consider preposterous quantities".*

On average, the adult working male ate 6.4 kg (one stone) of potatoes per day. Adult females ate 5.1 kg per day. The potatoes were eaten in three equal meals for breakfast, dinner and supper.

Table 1: Potato consumption per day

(Labourers, cottiers and smallholders families)	
Adult Male	6.4 kg (14 lb)
Adult Female	5.1 kg (11.2 lb)
Children 11-15 years	5.1 kg (11.2 lb)
Children under 11 years	2.2 kg (4.9 lb)

It should be noted that not everyone depended exclusively on the potato. The better off farmers, non-agricultural workers and the higher classes consumed a more varied diet of potatoes, bread, milk, eggs, meat, etc.. Also, in some parts of the country, mainly Ulster and North Leinster, oatmeal was a major constituent of the diet (Figure 4). In those areas about one-third less potatoes were consumed even by the poorer classes. The potatoes were replaced in the diet by stirabout (porridge) and bread.

Figure 4: Distribution of oatmeal eating areas prior to the Famine

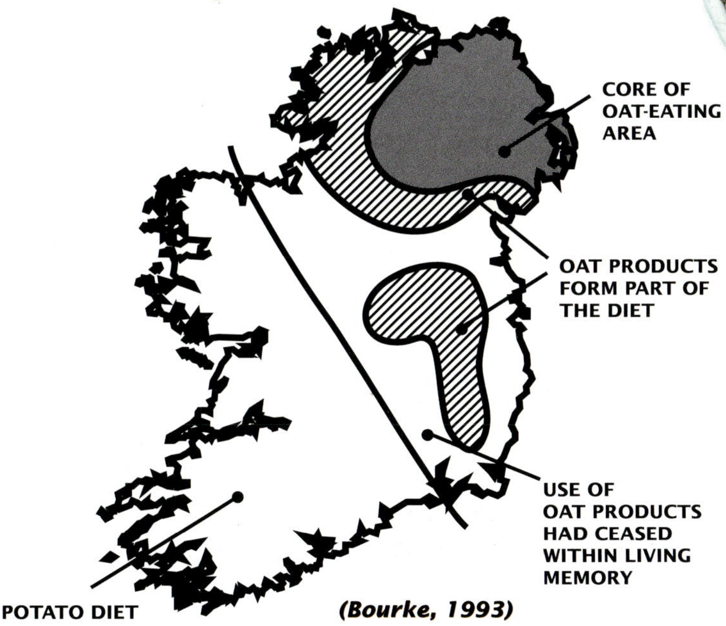

The Lumper was the most widely grown potato variety in pre-Famine Ireland.

The Poor and the Potato

For poor families, potatoes were an excellent subsistence crop:

- One hectare of potatoes could produce as much food as two hectares of barley or three hectares of oats or wheat.
- Sowing and harvesting could be done after the small-holder or labourer had finished helping the landlord or farmer complete their work.
- Potatoes could be grown on very poor quality land.
- Surplus potatoes could be fed to pigs and poultry. The money made from the sale of the meat or eggs was essential to the survival of the poor.

The main disadvantage of the "Potato Economy" and of subsistence living on potatoes was that if the crop failed, families had no resources to fall back on.

The Potato as a Food

Potatoes contain carbohydrates, protein, fats, minerals and vitamins (Table 2). Together with milk or buttermilk they provided a balanced if monotonous diet. Visitors to the country at the time confirmed this and reported that, despite the poverty, the people were well fed, healthy and athletic in appearance. Army and navy recruitment records for the period also confirmed that Irish recruits were taller than their English and Welsh counterparts.

The high nutritional content of the potato prevented scurvy (marked by bleeding and sponginess of the gums and caused by lack of vitamin C), pellagra (marked by shrivelled skin and wasted body) and xerophthalmia (eye disease due to deficiency of vitamin A), common scourges of the poor in other countries at that time.

- Potato starch is digested slowly, so the energy is used as it is released, rather than being stored.
- Potatoes contain a small amount of high quality protein. When consumed in large quantities this becomes a major source of protein.
- Dietary fibre more than doubles when the potato skins are also consumed.

Table 2: Nutritive value of boiled potatoes (per 100kg)

Energy value (kJ)	343
Complex carbohydrate (g)	19.7
Protein (g)	1.4
Fat	Trace
Vitamin C (mg)	4-14
Dietary fibre (g)	1.0

Living Standards

Living and housing conditions in the period before the Famine were very variable. The rich lived in high quality Class 1 houses while the poor lived in Class 4 cabins.

The quality of house in which a family lived was a reflection of their standard of living.

Classes of Houses

4th Class Houses
One roomed cabin or hovel
Labourers

3rd Class Houses
Two to four rooms with windows
Cottiers and small farmers

2nd Class Houses
5 - 9 rooms with windows
Large farmers

1st Class Houses
All better than Class 2
Landlords and gentry.

The census of 1841 showed that nearly half of all rural families were living in one roomed cabins (Class 4 houses). In Co Kerry the percentage was as high as 67%, while in the Barony of Beara it was 81% (Figure 5).

Figure 5: Number of houses in each class category in 1841 and 1851 ('000).

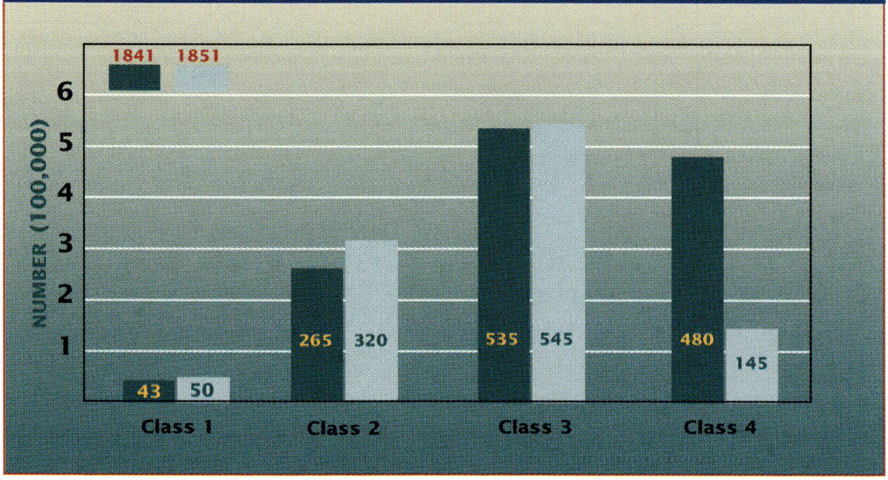

Example

In the parish of Cappamore, Co Limerick, there were 645 houses in 1841, 496 of these were Class 4 cabins. Between 1841 and 1851, 339 of the Class 4 cabins were knocked or closed, while the number of families living in Class 3 and Class 2 houses increased (Table 3). The Cappamore experience largely reflected the national situation where 70% (335,000) of the one roomed cabins were closed or knocked between 1841 and 1851, primarily as a result of the Famine.

People living in class four accommodation in 1841 were among those who suffered most during the Famine.

Table 3: Number of houses in each class category in Cappamore, Co Limerick 1841 and 1851

	Total	*Class 1*	*Class 2*	*Class 3*	*Class 4*
1841	645	8	29	112	496 (77%)
1851	424	7	65	195	157 (36%)

Source: Cappamore: A Parish History

The Cabins of the Poor

The poor built and repaired their own houses, normally without assistance from the landlord. There was little inducement to build houses to last for longer than the lease term (31 years, 21 years or at will) as there was no compensation paid should the family have to move when the lease was up.

The cabins were built from whatever materials were available in the vicinity.

> *'Their clay or stone walls gathered from the earth on the spot, their timbers dug from the bogs, their thatch harvested from the fields'*
>
> ***E Estyn Evans, Irish Folk Ways.***

A reconstructed Famine house, Knockfierna Hill, Ballingarry, Co. Limerick.

Doors were kept narrow and low, while window openings were narrow, placed high in the walls and widened internally. A timber frame, a bundle of straw or a dried sheepskin served as a substitute for glass. Thick coats of limewash applied annually gave protection to the mud wall houses.

The roof was constructed of rafters, sticks, sods and thatch. The sods were laid on the roof, grass upwards and were thatched with straw, rushes or reeds.

The fire was at floor level on a stone slab and the area around the fire was often paved. The wall behind the fire was protected by a flagstone. The fire served to prepare the food, dry clothes, keep the family warm and the thatch dry. In many cabins there was no chimney but a hole in the roof above the fire served to let out the smoke. The fire was looked after by the woman of the house and the children.

There was very little furniture. Stools and benches were most common. Fireside seats were often merely a stone or a block of wood. All seating was low in order to keep the inhabitants below the smoke which filled the cabin from the roof downwards. Where used, kitchen tables were placed along the wall.

The centre of the room and the space in front of the fire was kept open. This was where the family slept with their feet to the fire, lying on rushes or straw and covered with blankets or dry clothes.

The squalor in which the poor lived was vividly described by visitors to Ireland in the years before the Famine.

> *"One single room contains the father, mother and children and sometimes a grandfather or grandmother. There is no furniture in this wretched hovel, a single bed of hay or straw serves the entire family. Five or six half naked children may be crouched near a fire. In the midst of all this lies a pig, the only thriving inhabitant of this wretched habitation".*
>
> ***(Gustave de la Bonninieve de Beaumont: Friday, 27 Sept., 1839)***

> *Harry Kiogh's dwelling... "it is an old cow house... no window, no chimney, a sort of door that don't fit. I saw no bedclothes, straw below, a sort of old dark cloth above, there was a pot and a plate or two and a basin and spoon and the remains of an old dresser, four starved looking children, very clean ..."*
>
> ***(Journal of Elizabeth Smith, 1841)***

The Struggle for Survival

For the poorer section of the population life was an ongoing struggle. An insight into the harshness of the situation can be obtained from studying the Kiogh family budget for 1842 (Table 4).

To survive, and pay the rent, the family needed an income of about £8.00 per year. The rent for the cabin (already described) was £2.00 each year. A further £2.00 was required to rent conacre, although this sum did not rent sufficient land to grow potatoes to last the full year and so potatoes or oatmeal had to be purchased to keep the family alive between May and September. Money was also required to buy a pig for fattening, flax and wool for clothes, salt, soap, starch, herring and meat for Christmas and to pay the tailor and weaver.

Table 4: KIOGH FAMILY BUDGET, 1842
Parents and 4 children, landless labourers

	Expenditure	£	s.	d.		Income	£	s.	d.
Mar.	Rent of Cabin	1	0	0	Mar. to May	Wages-tilling and planting 60 @ 8d/day	2	0	0
	Rent of conacre	2	0	0					
	Wool, tow and flax for clothes		10	0					
May	Potatoes/oatmeal (Own exhausted in May)	1	0	0		Wages-Hay-making and harvesting	2	0	0
Sept.	Rent of Cabin	1	0	0		Sale of pig	2	10	0
	Purchase of Pig	1	0	0					
	Pay tailor, weaver and buy cloth		10	0		Sale of eggs, chickens, ducks, work if available	1	15	0
	Buy flax		5	0					
	Buy salt, soap, starch, herring and meat at Christmas	1	0	0					
		8	5	0			8	5	0

**240d = £1.00*

Based on the Journal of Elizabeth Smith and the Devon Committee Records

Family income came from working as a farm labourer at wages of 8d per day, in today's money 3.3 pence per day. However, sufficient work for all labourers was only available in the busy season, during sowing and harvesting, i.e. about 100-120 days per year. The sale of the pig brought in a further £2.50. Unless additional income could be generated from extra farm work, knitting or sewing or the sale of eggs, chickens, or ducks, the family would have to do without new clothes and/or go hungry for a period.

Land Tenure

The land was owned by an aristocracy/gentry class who often let it to middlemen. These set out to make a profit by subletting the land to tenants, smallholders and cottiers. In Ireland the land alone was let, buildings were not provided. This was different from the situation in England where land and buildings were let as a working unit. On leaving holdings, either because the lease was not renewed or the family could no longer pay the price asked, tenants (except in the North where it was the custom) were not compensated for improvements made.

As the population grew the demand for land increased. Landlords and middlemen availed of the opportunity to increase their income by allowing holdings to be divided and sub-divided and by letting holdings "at will". This reduced the security of tenants and enabled rents to be raised from year to year, a practice known as "rack-renting". The reality of the situation was the greater the number of smallholders the greater the income that could be derived from the land. The result by 1845 was a large number of small holdings — see Table 5.

The 505,000 cottiers and smallholders (under 10 acres) accounted for 1.75 million people in 1845. The largest and poorest group, the 650,000 landless labourers and their dependants accounted for a further 2.25 million people.

Table 5: Number of persons holding land, 1845

Acres	*Number*	*%*
Less than 1 acre	135,314	8.5
1 to 10	369,859	23.3
10 to 20	187,582	11.9
20 - 50	141,819	9.0
Above 50	70,441	4.4
Unclassified	30,433	1.9
Total landholders	935,448	59.0
Landless labourers	650,552	41.0
Total	**1,586,000**	**100.00**

1 hectare = 2.47 acres *Source: Bourke*

Eviction scene — tenants "at will" could be evicted if their rents were over 6 months in arrears. Note the troops in attendance.

Fear of Eviction

The majority of occupants were cottiers or tenants-at-will and they were always concerned about eviction:

- Leaseholders could be evicted if their rents were over 12 months in arrears.
- Tenants-at-will could be evicted if their rents were over 6 months in arrears.
- Rents in the 1840s averaged £3.20-£3.95 per hectare (£1.30-1.60 per acre).

Conacre

The landless labourer depended on renting conacre to secure land for growing potatoes:

- Land was let for a single season.
- The highest rents were paid for potato ground, particularly where it was manured. Prices of £4, £6, and even £8 per acre (0.4 hectare) were recorded.
- Rents were often paid by the plotholder working for the farmer or landlord at rates of from 8d to 10d per day in lieu of wages.

It is estimated that about 140,000 hectares (350,000 acres) of land were let on the conacre system in 1845. However, this was only sufficient to provide potatoes from September to April/May for the 650,000 landless labourers and their families.

Land Use

Oats, potatoes, wheat and barley were the principle crops grown in pre-famine Ireland. In total, some 2.4 million hectares were sown under crops annually (Figure 6).

Spadesmen in Co. Waterford circa 1824. The one sided spades were known as "loys". The design varied greatly throughout the country. At the time almost all tillage work was done by hand.

Figure 6: Estimated crop areas in hectares, 1845 and 1992

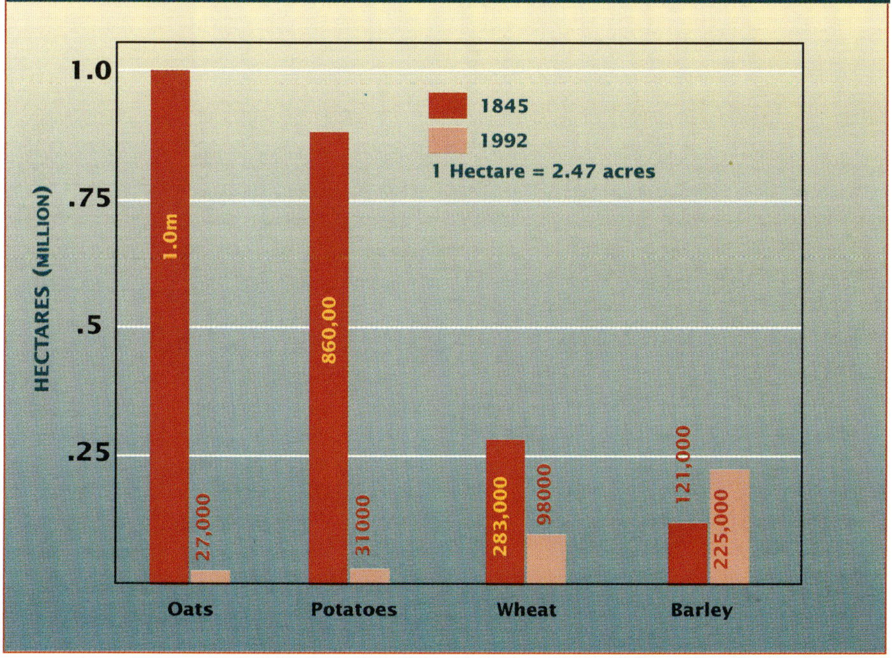

The scale of the work involved can only be understood by comparing the position with today. Nowadays less than 400,000 hectares of crops are grown and almost all the work is done by machinery. In the 1840s there was six times more tillage and almost all the work was done by hand.

Farmhouse in Co. Kerry, Feb. 1846. The remaining potatoes are stored in a loft above the fireplace.

Two out of every three persons working in Ireland in 1841 were working on the land, today less than one in seven work on the land. At the time, only one in seven of the population lived in towns and cities, today four out of seven people live in towns and cities with a population of over 1,500.

On most farms the grain grown - oats, wheat and barley was not for consumption on the farm but for sale to pay the rent and tithes. Exports of corn to Britain increased each year from 1815 to 1845. By 1845 one quarter of grain output and one half of livestock output was exported, providing enough food for over two million people. It is estimated that approximately 3.25 million quarters of corn, 480,000 pigs, 260,000 sheep and 180,000 cattle were exported in 1845. Quarters of wheat, oats and barley weighed 214, 142 and 184kg, respectively.

Crop Yields

Great care was lavished on the potato crop and yields obtained at about 15 tonnes per hectare were excellent for that period. Yields of oats and wheat were about 1,500 - 1,600 kg per hectare and yields of barley about 2,200 kg per hectare.

The cabin of J. Donoghue, a small farmer on the O'Connell estate in Co. Kerry, February, 1846.

Industrial Stagnation

The census of 1841 showed that only 32% of males were engaged in non-agricultural employment. The main non-agricultural occupations were:

Clothing workers	213,000
Carpenters, blacksmiths, stonemasons	158,000
Miscellaneous workers	115,000
Professional men and merchants	128,000
Paupers	5,000
Unclassified	129,000

Except for the linen industry in Ulster, most of the other industries — wool, cotton, brewing, declined or stagnated after the end of the Napoleonic Wars. Industrial employment was therefore not an option open to rural labourers and small holders in the years before the Famine.

The town of Kilrush, Co. Clare.

Emigration

It is estimated that up to 1.5 million people emigrated from Ireland between 1812 and 1845. The main destinations were Britain, America and Canada with about one-third going to each country.

The majority of pre-famine emigrants were from Ulster and Leinster. They could speak English and were better off than people in the South and West. Many were also non-Catholic and so did not face the same level of discrimination. In this period, male emigrants outnumbered female emigrants by two to one.

Despite the numbers involved, pre-famine emigration did not lead to improved economic conditions.

On board an emigrant ship in the 1840s.

Chapter 2

The Potato in Ireland

The Potato In Ireland

The potato first came to Ireland about 1586. There are a number of theories as to how it arrived. One attributes the introduction to Sir Francis Drake who spent about two years hiding in "Drakes Pool" outside Crosshaven, Co Cork on his return from South America. There is also a belief that the potato came from a Spanish Armanda vessel shipwrecked off the Galway coast in 1588. However, the most widely accepted theory attributes the introduction of the potato to Sir Walter Raleigh. He owned a large estate around Youghal and was Mayor of Youghal from 1588 to 1590, around the time the potato was first introduced.

The first official record of the potato in Ireland is to be found in the Montgomery Manuscripts which refer to potatoes being grown in County Down in 1606. There are also many other reference to the potato which suggest that within 50 to 60 years of its introduction the potato was widely grown and had become an important supplementary food.

Sir Walter Raleigh

The potato rapidly became popular because:

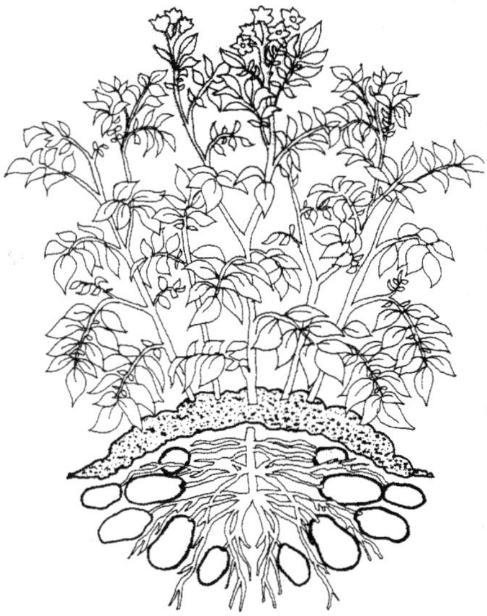

1. The soil and climate (wet and overcast) of Ireland were ideal for the potato.
2. The potato was easy to grow, easy to store, highly productive and required the minimum of cultivation and little investment.
3. The widespread misery of the people following the Battle of Kinsale, 1601, and its aftermath minimised the normal prejudice to a new food crop.
4. The potato is credited with saving Ireland from famine in 1629/30 and again during the Cromwellian War of 1645-1652.

Lazy Beds

The "lazy bed" system of growing potatoes was developed in the 1660s. The system had distinct advantages in wet and poorly drained soils and for a long time was also used to over-winter the potatoes. All the cultivation was done by hand and a spade referred to as a "loy" was used to prepare the lazy beds.

Figure 7: Construction of Lazy Beds.

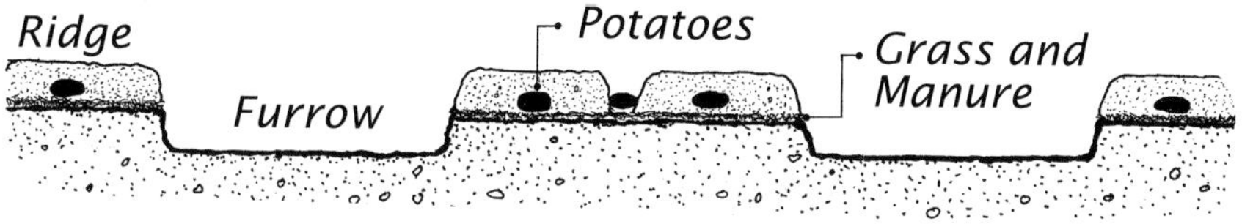

Above: A cross section of a lazy bed before the soil is spread accross from the furrow.
Below: Turning the sod with the loy.

Technique

- A grass sod measuring 27 cm wide, 8 cm deep and 35 cm long was turned onto the grass sward. Another sod was turned opposite this leaving a 10cm gap, manure was applied before the sods were turned.
- The gap in the middle of the ridge was covered with soil from the furrow.
- Three rows of potatoes were planted on the ridge in a diamond shape.
- Planting was usually done by the women. When the shoots were well grown, the potatoes were earthed up with 7cm of soil from the furrows.

Planting

Planting was done in April/May. Approximately 1250 - 1500 kg of cut seed (cut with eyes being left on both halves) or 2.5 tonnes of uncut seed was required to plant one hectare of potatoes.

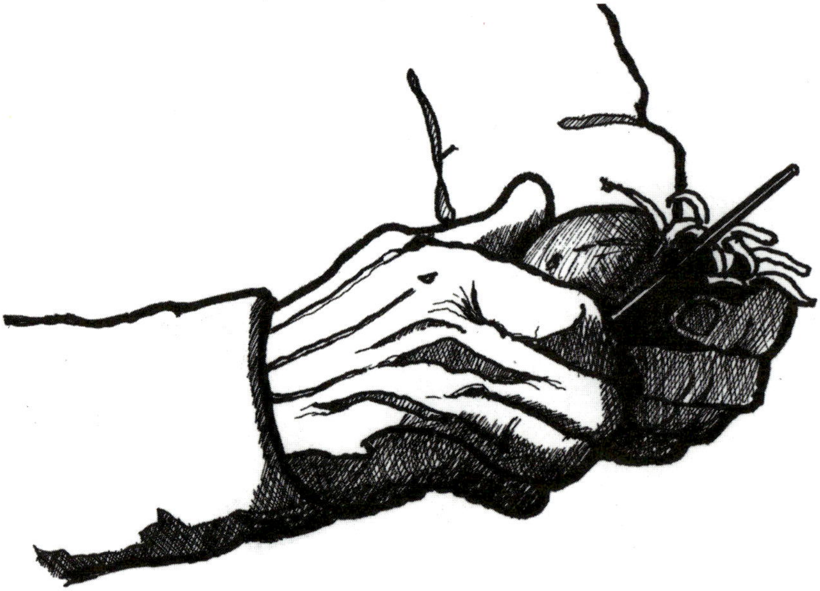

The potatoes were cut with eyes being left in both halves.

Pre-Famine Varieties

There were four outstanding pre-famine potato varieties: the Black, the Apple, the Cup and the Lumper.

The Black
(pre 1730)

This was a white fleshed variety with a black skin. It gave a good yield for the time and stored well into the following year.

The Apple
(1768)

This round red potato variety was noted for its mealy texture and excellent keeping quality.

The Cup
(pre 1808)

This variety was decribed as "more difficult to digest" than the Apple. However, it produced a 10 - 15% higher yield than the Apple and also grew well in upland areas.

The Lumper
(1808)

This white skinned, white fleshed variety produced high yields of knobbly potatoes. It gave 10-15% higher yield than the Cup and was first introduced for animal feed. Soon it became the most widely grown variety and accounted for almost 90 per cent of potatoes grown in the 1840s.

The Black *The Apple*

The Cup *The Lumper*

Manuring the Potatoes

Manure was crucial for a good yield of potatoes. With families depending on their potato crops for survival, every available material was used to build up an adequate manure heap over the summer and winter. Seaweed was harvested and hauled up to 30 miles inland. Spoil was collected from the roads and manure from pigs, poultry and animals was carefully husbanded. All family members were involved in the task. Other crops grown - oats, barley and wheat - subsequently benefited from the manure and care given to the potatoes.

Chapter 3

Blight

Blight

First reports of a new disease which affected the potato crop came from the Boston/New York area of the USA in 1843. The disease was brought across the Atlantic on tubers, imported into Belgium, for planting as seed in 1844. While the blight did not affect the potato crop in 1844, the disease spread rapidly in 1845 (Figure 8)

Spread of Blight in Europe

June	Blight identified in Belgium
Mid-July	All over Flanders and parts of Holland and France
Mid-August	Paris and Southern England
August 20th	Identified in Ireland

Figure 8: The spread of potato blight in Europe in 1845.

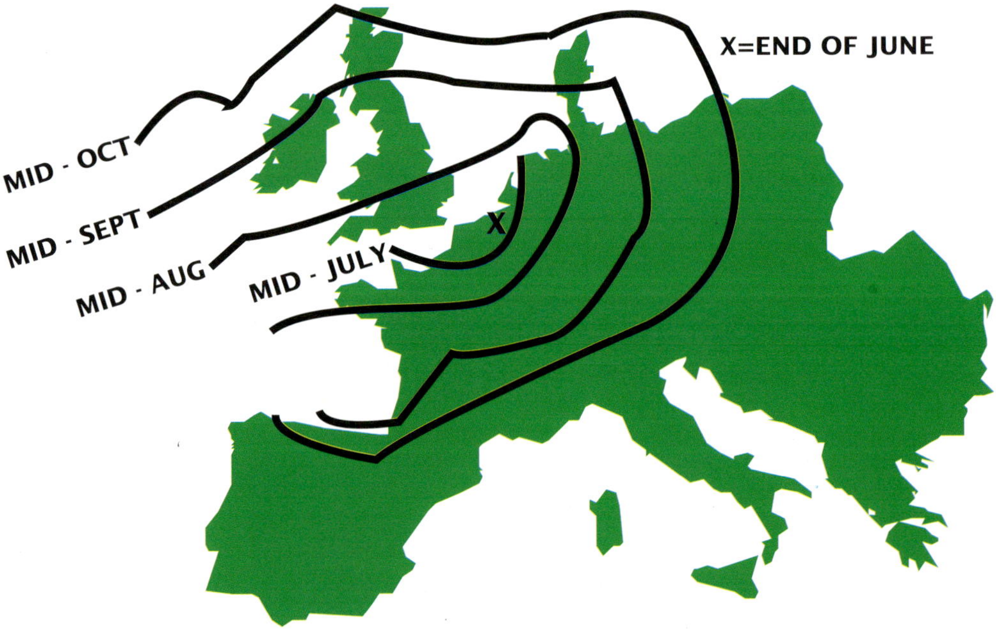

After Bourke and Dowley

What is Blight?

Blight is a fungus disease which attacks the leaves and tubers of the potato plant. It can be spread by spores in the air and spreads most rapidly in humid, mild weather.

Blight first appears as a small dark spot on the upper surface of the potato leaf. A corresponding whitish grey fungal growth is usually found on the underside of the leaf. Under favourable weather conditions the spot will enlarge and other infection spots appear. Eventually the entire plant is affected and it starts to wilt into a decaying mass giving off the easily recognised blight odour. With continued rainfall, the spores are washed off the plant and onto the tubers in the soil. When harvested these tubers begin to rot.

Blight first appears as dark spots on the leaves of the potato plant.

Partially infected seed tubers carry the disease through the winter and into the following spring. When planted, these seed tubers produce infected plants which restart the disease cycle. When cut in half, infected tubers show a reddish brown area underneath the skin.

Blight in Ireland

> *"We stop the press with very great regret to announce that the potato murrain has unequivocally declare itself in Ireland. The crops about Dublin are suddenly perishing ... where will Ireland be in the event of a universal potato rot?*
>
> ***Dr Lindly, Editor, Gardeners Chronicle, 13 September 1845.***

The Government sought to establish the extent of the crop loss. The following are typical of extracts from the Constabulary Reports for November, 1845.

Donegal	November 12	The disease is increasing fast, particularly in the pits. The farmers are generally trying the suggestions of the Commissioners.
Tipperary	November 12	The disease has spread extensively in the pits, a large portion of the potatoes pitted as sound 3 or 4 weeks ago being now bad and in some instances unfit for any use. On the lowest calculation, one third of the entire crop is diseased.
Kildare	November 13	Since the fall of rain, the crop is rapidly running to decay. The poorer class of people are beginning to despair

Source: Public Records Office of Ireland as quoted by Helen Litton, 1994.

Dying foliage in a potato crop severely affected by blight

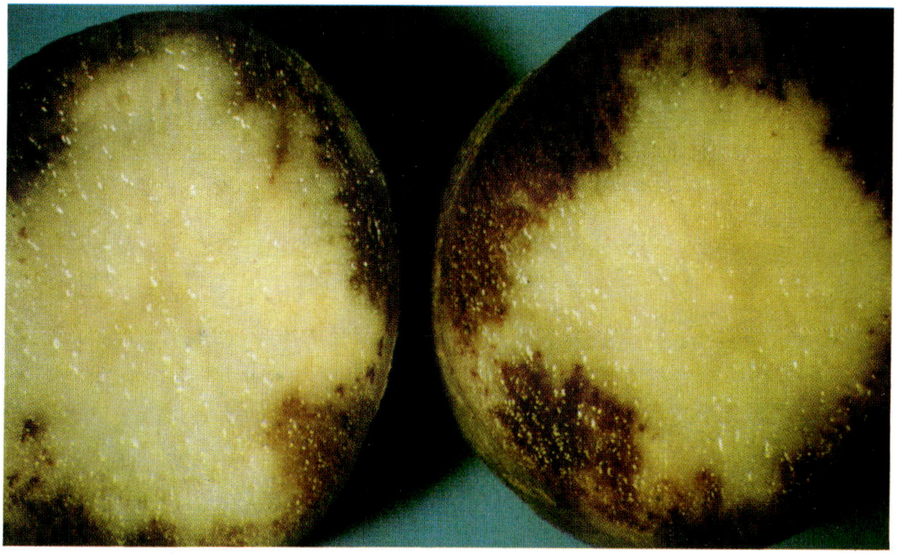

Tubers infected with blight; note the reddish brown marking underneath the skin.

Effect of Blight on the Potato Crop

1845 The late arrival of the blight reduced its spread in 1845. While potato rot caused the loss of about 40% of the crop it had yielded remarkably well and the shortfall was about 30% below normal.

1846 Plantings were down to about 0.5 million hectares. Blight stuck in July and the whole crop was destroyed by early August. Yields were less than 10% of normal or one months supply.

1847 Seed was very scarce and expensive. Less than 100,000 hectares were planted. The crop flourished and quality was good, but the Famine continued because of the small area planted.

1848 Great efforts and sacrifices were made to obtain seed and about 300,000 hectares were planted. Blight struck again in mid-July and the crop was destroyed in a few weeks.

1849 About 260,000 hectares were planted. Blight caused little loss and in the autumn of 1849 the Famine was officially at an end.

The extent of the loss of the potato crop in the Famine years 1845 to 1849 is summarised in Figure 9.

Figure 9: Extent of the potato loss triggered by blight during the Famine, 1845-1849

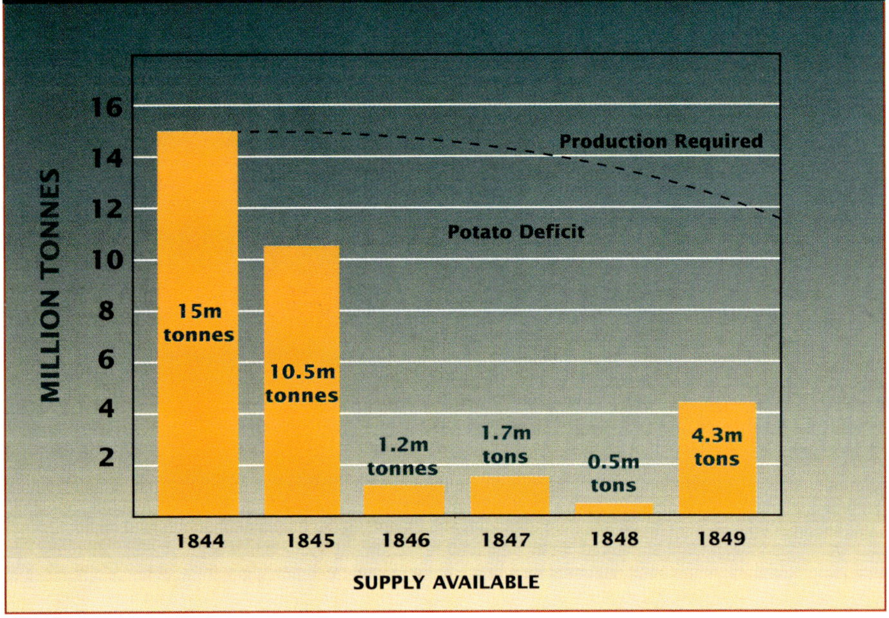

Chapter 4

Government Relief Schemes

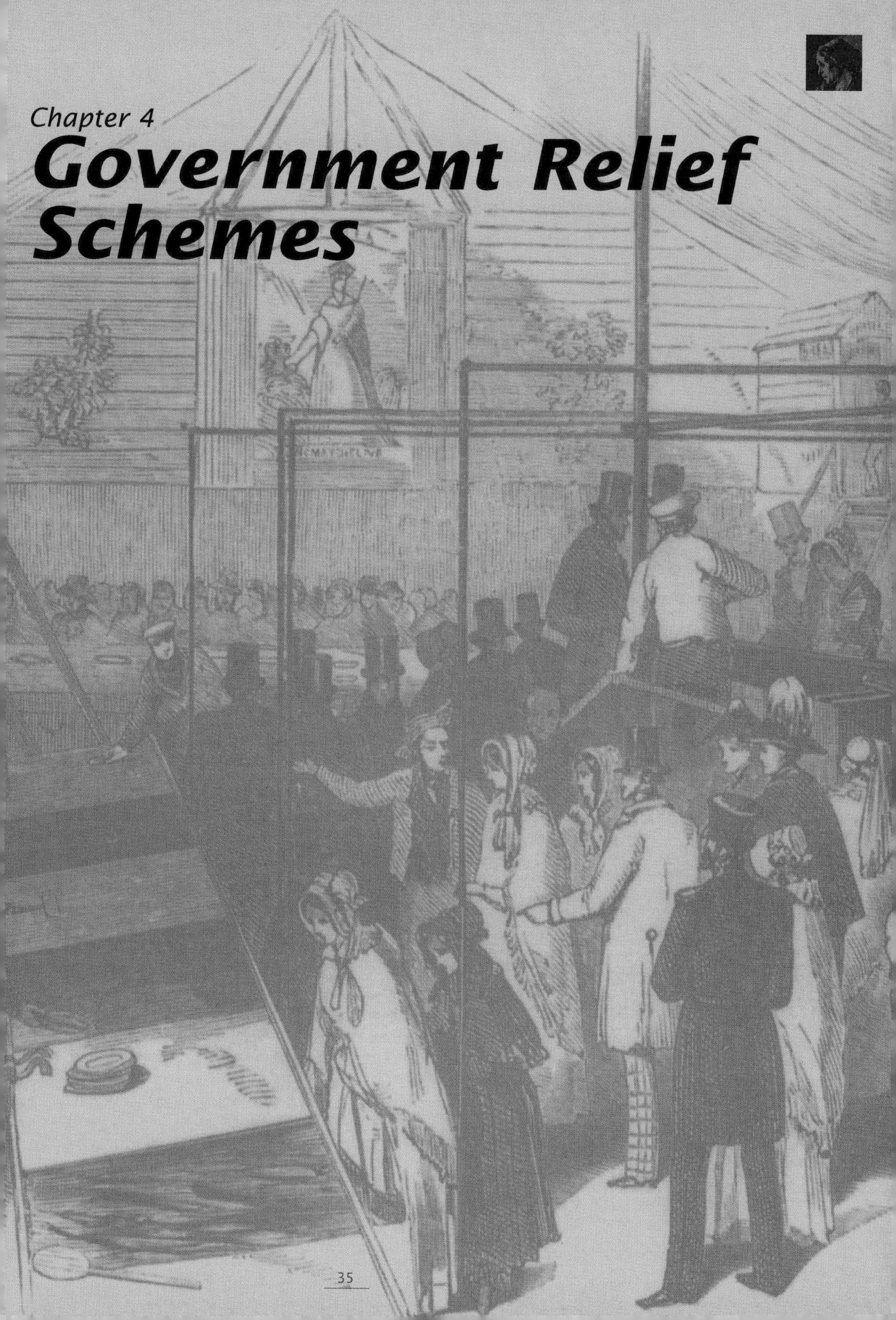

Government Relief Schemes

Partial loss of the potato crop was nothing new in Ireland. Localised losses had occurred in 1822, 1831, 1835, 1837 and 1839. To relieve the resulting distress, the destitute were usually employed in constructing roads and other public relief works. Collections were also organised to raise money to buy food for distribution.

In the autumn of 1845, appeals for relief measures to be introduced arrived to the authorities in Dublin and London from all over Ireland. The Prime Minister, Sir Robert Peel, had previously worked in Ireland and was determined to provide help. Everyone expected that the relief would only be required for a short period until the next potato harvest became available.

Peel's Relief Scheme

In November 1845, Sir Robert Peel, without awaiting Treasury approval, ordered £100,000 to be spent on buying Indian corn (maize) in the United States. He chose Indian corn because it had not previously been traded in Ireland and it would not interfere with the existing trade in cereals. His plan was to hold the corn in reserve to help stabilise grain prices.

The Indian Corn was not well received by the people. It was flint hard and difficult to grind in the flour mills of the time and was referred to disparagingly as "Peel's Brimstone". Soon, however, the people became familiar with the grain and it was in strong demand.

Sir Robert Peel

While there were widespread reports of great suffering in the months of March, April and May 1846, the relief measures put in place by Sir Robert Peel helped to avert deaths.

Relief Scheme 1845/46

Plan	*Outcome*
1.Set up Relief Commission	
a: raise subscriptions to purchase food	a: £98,000 collected by July 31, 1846 and £65,915 was added by the Exchequer.
b: establish food depots	b: food depots opened May 15, supplies quickly exhausted (ordered to close August 15).
c: persuade landlords to increase employment	
2. Commence Public Works to Increase Employment (costs to be paid by government- half costs being a grant, half a loan repayable over 20 years)	Works were undertaken in many areas despite delays and problems (instructed to close on August 15).
3. Purchase Indian Corn (maize)	£100,000 worth purchased. The maize helped keep food prices down and was almost the only food available from the food depots.
4. Repeal the Corn Laws - to enable grain to be imported freely	Law repealed on 25 June, 1846 but the bitter opposition to the proposal led to the fall of Peel's Government on 29 June, 1846.

Signing a petition against the repeal of the Corn Laws.

All expenditure needed for Famine relief in Ireland required the sanction of Charles Edward Trevelyan, Assistant Secretary of the Treasury. When the Tories (Conservatives) were voted out of the office in June 1846, Sir Robert Peel resigned as Prime Minister. Trevelyan, however, continued in his post in the Treasury under the new Whig (Liberals) Government. When in opposition, the Whigs had opposed Peel's relief scheme. As the Famine progressed, the Government became more restrictive and rigid in providing relief.

New Whig Government (Deciding Ireland's Fate)

Lord John Russell

Lord John Russell,
Prime Minister, 1846-1852

Retained responsibility for Irish policy. On his previous record it was assumed that he would be sympathetic to Ireland. His election was supported by Daniel O'Connell and other Irish Members of Parliament.

Charles Wood,
Chancellor of the Exchequer

Was a firm believer in "laissez faire" and was strongly against any measures involving new expenditure or new taxes.

Charles Wood

Charles Edward Trevelyan

Charles Edward Trevelyan,
Assistant Secretary of the Treasury

A capable official of strong character, he became virtual director of Irish Famine relief efforts. Trevelyan did not have a particular regard for the Irish, was very rigid in regard to Treasury rules and regulations and as the Famine progressed, developed policies to economise on Treasury expenditure.

Laissez Faire (let be)

The new government, like most politicians of the time, were fervent believers in the virtues of free enterprise. This, the dominant economic philosophy of the time, held that ...

"...it was not the government's role to interfere with the free market of goods or services or to provide aid for the people."

The politicians and officials were always concerned that government action would be ridiculed for interfering with private enterprise and commerce. Thus, when in July 1846 Trevelyan was informed that "disease is reappearing" he considered that the only way to stop the people "becoming habitually dependent on government" was to close and reorganise the Relief Scheme.

The Potato Fails Again

The speed with which the potato crop was destroyed in 1846 was described in a letter from Fr Mathew to Trevelyan.

"On the 27th (July) I passed from Cork to Dublin and this doomed plant bloomed in all the luxuriance of an abundant harvest. Returning on the 3rd (August) I beheld with sorrow one wide waste of putrefying vegetation. In many places the wretched people were seated on the fences of their decaying gardens, wringing their hands and wailing bitterly at the distraction that had left them foodless".

Fr Mathew, Cork to Trevelyan, August 7, 1846

The second failure of the potato crop in 1846 spread fear among the population.

The blight struck when the potato tubers were no bigger than marbles and yields were no more than one-tenth of normal, just enough to feed the population for one month. The people were in despair and once more turned to those in authority for help.

The blight was much more severe in Ireland than in Britain or Europe in 1846 (Figure 11). Throughout Europe, however, the grain harvest was poor and there was a general shortage of food. While the British Government put its faith in "laissez faire", the Governments of France, Belgium, etc bought any food supplies available. Soon food prices began to rise dramatically and the poor faced a winter of crisis.

Relief Scheme 1846/47

In the Government's relief scheme for 1846/47 great emphasis was placed on public works. The idea was to provide employment through which the destitute could earn wages to buy food. To fund the scheme, the Treasury agreed to advance the money needed, but the full cost of work undertaken was to be repaid from local rates over 10 years. Despite this, numerous schemes were submitted for the approval of the Board of Works.

Figure 11: Severity of potato blight in Europe in 1846.

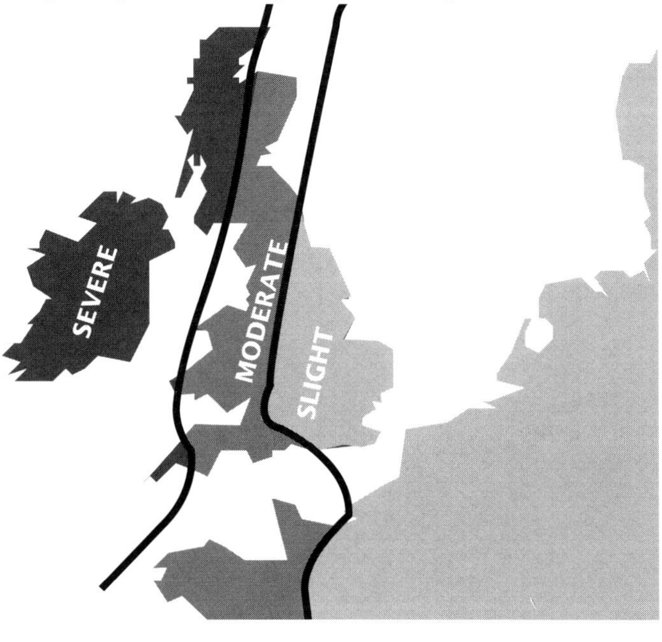

(After Bourke and Lamb)

Russell's Relief Scheme 1846/47

1. Public Works

Public works to continue but to be funded locally. Treasury would advance money to be repaid over 10 years.
(Labour Rate Act, Aug. 1846)

There were delays in getting work approved and in starting projects but numbers employed grew rapidly.

30,000 September
150,000 October
285,000 November
450,000 December
570,000 January
700,000 February
734,000 March

Despite the high numbers employed from December onwards, not all the destitute could get work, and with high food prices, the wages paid at 10d a day only provided one meal for a family of six. Instructions to start closing the public works were issued on March 10, 1847

2. Food Supply

Government would undertake not to import or supply any food

When enquiries were eventually made in October 1846, supplies were unavailable because of the poor harvest throughout Europe.

3. Food Depots

Food depots would be established in the West

Were never adequately supplied. Did not open until 28 December 1846 and then only to sell food at market prices plus 5%.

Throughout the autumn and winter of 1846/47, the number of destitute pleading for employment on the public works continued to increase. In December 1846 over £540,000 was paid out in wages, yet it had little impact on conditions. Gradually the people on the public works became too weak to work, many were dressed in rags and they faced the most severe winter in memory. In addition, the wages earned were insufficient to buy enough food to feed a family.

With wages at 8d to one shilling per day - less food could be bought as prices rose

In January 1847 the Government decided that due to the high costs involved (almost £5m in the autumn and winter of 1846/47) and the need for people to work the land, relief by employment was to be abandoned. In its place the Soup Kitchen Act was introduced on January 25, 1847.

Famine wall (1847), Charleville Estate, Tullamore, Co. Offaly. Employment was only given to those with tickets from local relief committees.

Soup Kitchen Act

Under the Act, soup kitchens were to be established in each of the 2,049 electoral divisions. The costs involved were to be paid for out of Irish rates and subscriptions. The ratepayers opposed the Act because rates had already increased from 5d in the pound to 1s 8d in the pound since the Famine began.

By May 1847 some 1,250 soup kitchens and by June some 1,850 were in operation. Although only cooked food was served, and the people regarded public queuing with containers as degrading, over 3 million people were collecting rations daily by July 1847. Soon instructions to close the soup kitchens were issued. Those in 55 of the 130 Unions (workhouse areas) closed

on 15 August, those in 29 Unions closed on 12 September and in 49 Unions on 31 October, 1847. Total cost was about £1.75 million.

Soup Ingredients

Soup issued could include any food cooked in a boiler and distributed in a liquid state, whether thick or thin. The recommended daily ration was one quart (2 pints) of soup thickened with meal and 4 oz of bread. Children under nine years of age got a half ration. The following were among the recipes used.

Soyer's Soup

This recipe was developed by Alexis Soyer, a famous French chef of the Reform Club in London.

¼ lb leg of beef
2 gallons of water
2 oz dripping
2 onions and other vegetables
½ lb flour (seconds)
½ lb pearl barley
3 oz salt
½ oz brown sugar

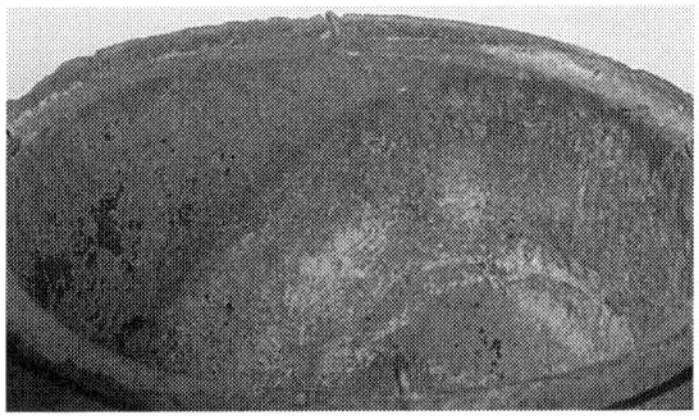

A pot used at Ballyumber, Co. Offaly for boiling soup during the Famine.

Soyer claimed that a meal of his soup once a day, together with a biscuit was sufficient to sustain the strength of a strong and healthy man.

Mrs Neale's Soup

Recipe used by Mrs Neale, Castleconnel, Co Limerick

30 lb beef
8 lb barley
8 lb steeped peas
2 stone turnips
5d worth leeks and other vegetables
190 quarts water

Interior view of the soup kitchen operated by The Society of Friends, Cork, 1847.

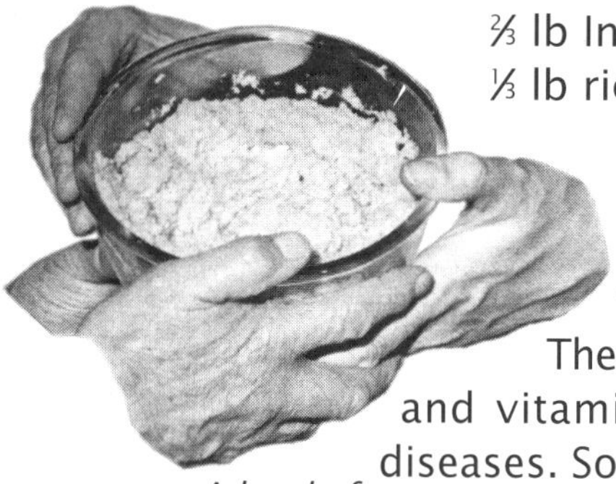

A bowl of stirabout.

Stirabout

⅔ lb Indian meal
⅓ lb rice (when obtainable)

This mixture when cooked with water as "stirabout" or porridge swelled into a ration weighing 3 to 5 lb (1.3 to 2.3 kg) in weight.

The soup recipes were generally not balanced for minerals and vitamins and over time gave rise to scurvy and other diseases. Some were also too thin (watery) leading to diarrhoea.

Grattan's Soup

The following recipe was used on the estate of the Right Hon. James Grattan, Vicarstown, Co Laois.

1 ox head without tongue
28 lb turnips
3½ lb onions
7 lb carrots
21 lb pea-meal
14 lb Indian meal
30 gallons water

Chapter 5

The Famine 1845-1849

The Famine 1845-1849

A mother in Clonakilty begging for money to buy a coffin to bury her dead child.

Reports of distress and deaths quickly followed the second failure of the potato crop in 1846. Soon the people were scavenging the countryside for anything that could be eaten. Nettles, dandelions, roots and berries were eaten, rabbits, foxes, hares and birds were trapped for food. Pigs, poultry (where available), cats and dogs were also used for food. Nothing however, except massive supplies of grain, could replace the loss of the potato crop and the slide to famine continued unabated.

Eyewitness accounts from the period help convey the hardship and suffering experienced.

"...the children are like skeletons, their features sharpened with hunger and their limbs wasted... the happy expression of infancy gone from their faces, leaving the anxious look of premature old age"

William Elliot Foster, Society of Friends, reporting from Carrick-on-Shannon, December, 1846

"I went on the 15th (December) to Skibbereen... being aware that I should have to witness scenes of frightful hunger, I provided myself with as much bread as five men would carry, and on reaching the spot I was surprised to find the wretched hamlet apparently deserted. I entered some of the hovels to ascertain the cause, and the scenes which presented themselves were such as no tongue or pen can convey the slightest idea of.

In the first, six famished and ghastly skeletons, to all appearances dead, were huddled in a corner on some filthy straw, their sole covering what seemed a ragged horsecloth, their wretched legs hanging about, naked above the knees. I approach with horror, and found by a low moaning they were alive - they were in fever, four children, a woman and what had once been a man. It is impossible to go through the detail. Suffice

it to say that in a few minutes I was surrounded by at least 200 such phantoms, such frightful spectres as no words can describe, either from famine or from fever. Their demoniac yells are still ringing in my ears, and their horrible images are fixed upon my brain. My heart sickens at the recital, but I must go on.

In another case, decency would forbid what follows, but it must be told. My clothes were nearly torn off in my endeavour to escape from the throng of pestilence around, when my neckcloth was seized from behind by a grip which compelled me to turn, I found myself grasped by a woman with an infant just born in her arms and the remains of a filthy sack across her loins - the sole covering of herself and her baby. The same morning the police opened a house on the adjoining lands, which was observed shut for many days and two frozen corpses were found lying upon the mud floor, half devoured by rats".

Mr Nicholas Cummins,
Cork Magistrate in a letter published in The Times,
December 24, 1846

The Mullins' hut at Schull - one child sick on the bed, three huddle silently around the fire.

Mr Richard Inglis investigating the situation for the Government confirmed: *"deaths were occurring daily, 197 persons had died in the workhouse since November 5, and nearly 100 bodies had been found dead in the lanes or in derelict cabins, half eaten by rats"*

Cecil Woodham-Smith, 1962

"After leaving Clonakilty we met a funeral or a coffin at every hundred yards until we approached Shepperton Lakes. Here the distress became more striking". (Illustrated London News, Feb 1847)

"I confess myself unmanned by the intensity and extent of the suffering I witnessed, more especially among the women and little children, crowds of whom were to be seen scattered over the turnip field, like a flock of famished crows, devouring the raw turnips, mothers half naked, shivering in the snow and sleet... their children screaming with hunger".

Captain Wynne, Board of Works, Co Clare, January 1847

"18,000 inhabited the parish, three quarters of that population were skeletons with swelling of the limbs and diarrhoea universal... in one cabin four adults and three children were crouched, silent, over a fire, while in another room a man and woman lay in bed,

mere skeletons. The son of these people had been on the public works and earned 8d a day, which was not enough to keep the family from starvation, and he himself was now ill from hunger. These had been a prosperous couple.

In a second cabin, a mother and daughter, reduced to skins stretched over bones, lay in bed. Both must be dead by this time. The third cabin contained an old woman and her daughter, whose husband had deserted her, with three little children. The grandmother had already died. The fourth cabin also contained a corpse which had been lying there for four days - no one could be found with sufficient strength to take it away"

Commander Caffyn, British navy, Schull, Co Cork, 15 February 1847

Searching for potatoes left behind in previously dug ground.

The destitute seeking admission to the workhouse. Artistic impression drawn after the Famine.

Uncoffin'd, unshrouded, his bleak corpse they bore,
From the spot where he died on the Cabin's wet floor,
To a hole which they dug in the garden close by;
Thus a brother hath died-thus a Christian must lie!

'Twas a horrible end and a harrowing tale,
To chill the strong heart-to strike revelry pale,
No disease o'er this Victim could mastery claim,
'Twas Famine alone mark'd his skeleton frame!

(C.C.T. Illustrated London News, 1847

Death claims another victim in 1847.

Trade in Food

Exports of grain continued throughout the Famine. The quantity exported declined from 513,000 tons in 1845 to 284,000 tons in 1846 and 146,000 tons in 1847 (Table 6). The grain was grown to pay the rent which forced the farmers to sell at the best price available.

To the starving population, food exports at a time of great want did not make sense. Attempts to prevent exports led to food riots and attacks on convoys moving grain to the ports. The Government refused to ban food exports and indeed sent

Table 6 : Grain imports and exports 1844 - 1848

Year	*Exports (tons)*	*Imports (tons)**
1844	424,000	30,000
1845	513,000	28,000
1846	284,000	197,000
1847	146,000	909,000
1848	314,000	439,000

**Mainly Indian meal (maize) and wheat.* *Source : Bourke, 1993*

2,000 additional troops to protect the grain trade. As the Famine progressed, grain imports far exceeded exports, particularly in 1847.

The 284,000 tons of grain exported in 1846 would not have prevented the famine as up to 3 million tons of grain was needed to compensate for the loss of the potato crop. It could however have provided 1 lb of meal per day for 4 million people for 160 days. This allowance would have greatly alleviated hardship while the country awaited supplies of Indian meal in the spring of 1847. There was, however, no one to organise the transaction between the farmers and the poor.

Dungarvan, Co. Waterford, the scene of food riots in 1847.

Trevelyan's Relief Schemes

Blight did not affect the potato crop in 1847, however, very few potatoes were grown, especially by the poor. Consequently, the people faced another winter of hunger at a time when British financial markets were in crisis. The subsequent Famine Relief Scheme for 1847/48 drawn up by Trevelyan set out to minimise costs to the Treasury. Under the scheme the destitute were to be transferred to the charge of the Irish Poor Law Commissioners and Irish Rates.

Relief Scheme 1847/48

- 22 of the 130 unions would be listed as "distressed" and could get assistance on costs from national funds *(see also Chapter 6).*
- Able-bodied only were to get relief within a workhouse.
- Non-able bodied could get relief outside the workhouses and retain their homes.
- All applicants were to be investigated.

Driving cattle, sheep and goats for rent. Landlords often seized stock in lieu of rent arrears.

The drive to collect rates to fund the scheme was relentless, *("rate collectors, aided by police, are out daily seizing wearing apparel and tools even")* and by December 1847, almost £1m had been collected.

By February 1848, 450,000 people and by June 830,000 people were receiving outdoor relief. Considering the distances people had to walk (food was only distributed at workhouses), the poor health of the people and spoiling of food on the journey home, the large numbers claiming relief demonstrated the level of distress. The "quarter acre clause" introduced in 1847 meant that smallholders, despite their level of destitution, could not claim relief unless they gave up their holdings. As a consequence families were starving to death rather than relinquishing their holdings and this clause was relaxed in May 1848.

Relief Scheme 1848/49

In the spring of 1848, the people made massive sacrifices to obtain seed potatoes - clothes, tables, chairs, etc were sold. However, the blight struck again and the crop was destroyed.

> *"On the morning of the 13th (July) to the astonishment of everyone, the potato fields that had on the previous evening presented an appearance that was calculated to gladden the hearts of the most indifferent, appeared blasted, withered, blackened, as it were, sprinkled with vitriol..."*
>
> ***Fr John O'Sullivan, Kenmare, July 16, 1848***

Wheat and corn crops were also poor. In 1848 in the midst of the resulting confusion and dismay, the Young Irelanders wanting immediate and radical solutions to Ireland's problems attempted insurrection. The result, a skirmish at the Widow McCormack's house in Ballingarry, Co Tipperary. The Prime Minister, Lord John Russell, was not amused and in reply to appeals for help stated that “generosity was hardly to be expected after an attempted insurrection”. Meanwhile Trevelyan was determined on a policy of ruthless economy and confirmed that:

- Higher rates were to be collected.
- There would be no Treasury grants to distressed unions.
- Unwanted clothing would not be issued to workhouses as previously.
- The outdoor feeding of destitute children was to stop to encourage independence.

Suffering and distress in the early months of 1849 were reported to be as bad as in 1847. The effects of the Famine were also cumulative and the people were described as “skinned down to the bone”.

The distress caused concern in Britain and a new Rate-in-Aid Act was passed. Under this Act, the more prosperous unions in Ireland were to contribute to the support of distressed unions.

Chapter 6

Private and Workhouse Relief Efforts

Private and Workhouse Relief Efforts

With the loss of the potato crop, the poor were penniless. Their plight led to the formation of private relief efforts.

Among the most notable were:

The Society of Friends (Quakers)

Relief provided had a total value of almost £200,000. The Quakers were among the first to set up soup kitchens and they were also involved in the importation of food supplies from the United States and in the distribution of clothing. They continued to operate soup kitchens up to June 1849 and made a major contribution to Famine relief efforts.

Captain Kennedy and his young daughter distributing clothes to the poor in Kilrush, Co. Clare. He was outspoken in his demands for more help for the poor. It eventually cost him his job and he emigated to England.

The British Association

Spent about £390,000 through existing relief committees. £160,000 was used in the Autumn of 1847 in supporting distressed unions, generally in the poorer parts of the country, to keep workhouses open and purchase food for the destitute within.

The Irish Relief Association

Collected up to £70,000.

The Ladies Work Association

Made clothes for the destitute.

The American Relief Committees

Collected subscriptions totalling about $1m and sent food aid.

St Vincent de Paul Society

Was active in several areas including Kilrush, Co Clare.

Others

Individual landlords, members of the clergy and notable persons also operated soup kitchens, collected subscriptions and distributed clothes. There were also donations from many other countries and groups.

International subscriptions for Irish Famine relief largely ceased in 1847. The duration of the crisis and irritation at the arrival of poor Irish immigrants among the donor populations caused a decline in sympathy.

Charitable Workers

Tribute must be paid to the courage of the many charitable workers who helped victims of the Famine. There were many deaths among the care workers - doctors, nurses, clergy of all denominations and volunteers. It is reported that the proportion of deaths among the upper classes who caught fever was higher than that among the general population.

Workhouses

A network of 130 workhouses, built under the Poor Law Act of 1838, were in place at the start of the Famine. They were run by Boards of Guardians and had space for about 100,000 people. They were built to provide refuge and shelter for the destitute, the sick, the insane and the old. Conditions in the workhouses were harsh and designed to ensure that only those in dire necessity would seek admission.

The Irish had a great dislike of the workhouse system and did not enter or remain there if at all possible. Even by August 1846, there were only about 43,000 inmates. However, as food

Figure 12: Poor Law Union Workhouses pre-1849 .

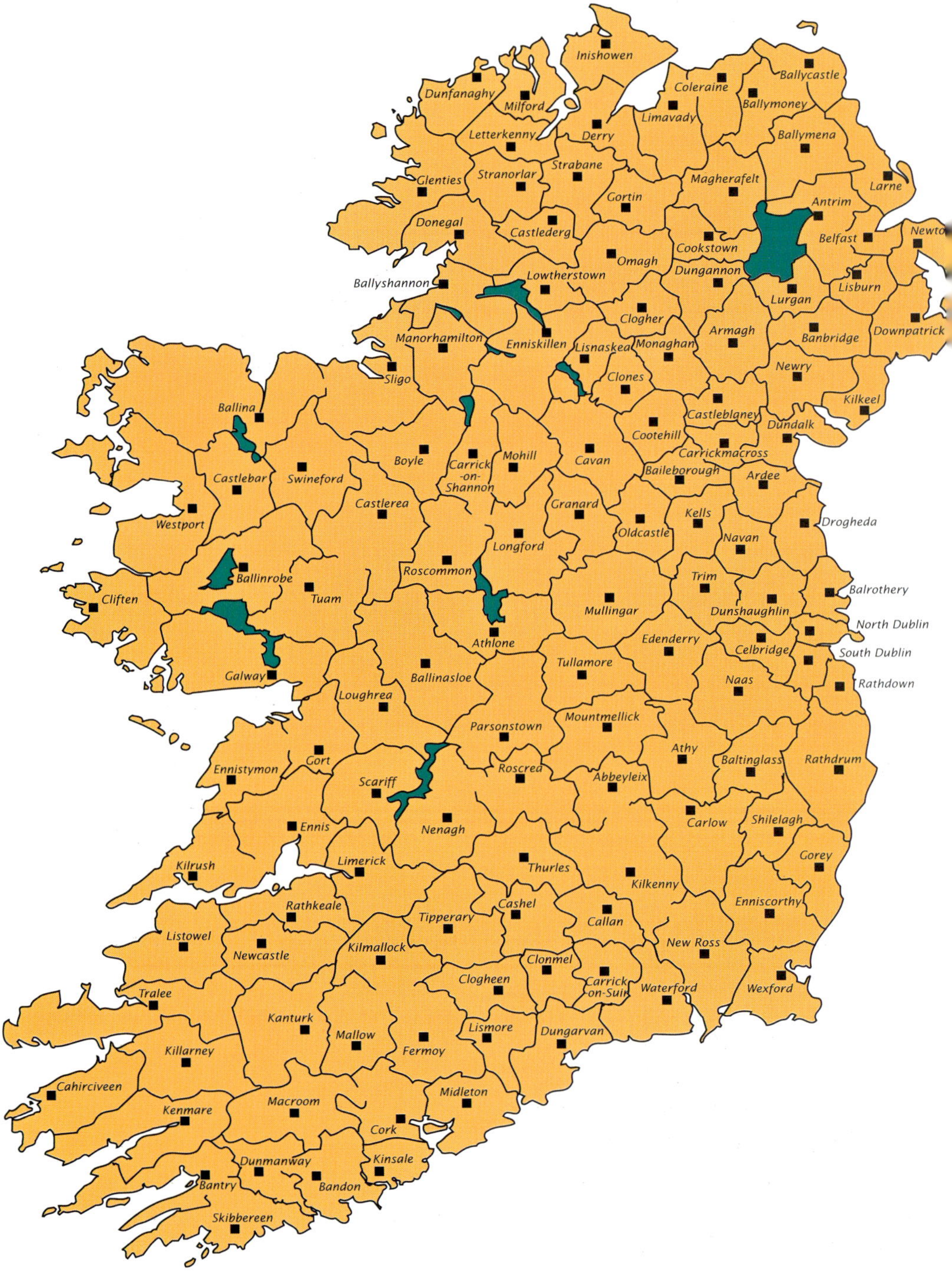

(Based on map by Paul Ferguson, Trinity College Dublin.)

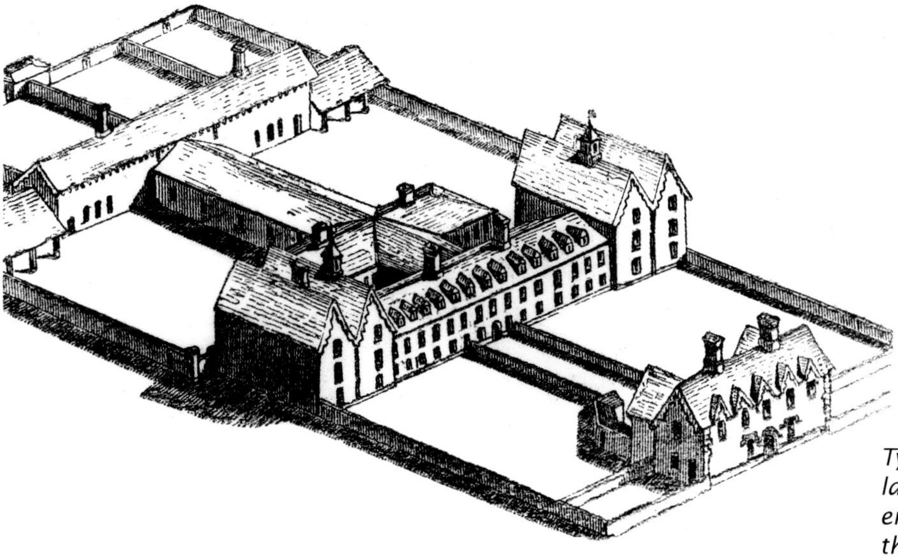

Typical workhouse layout, with the entrance block at the front

prices climbed in the Autumn of 1846, the people became desperate and numbers increased dramatically. Soon demand far exceeded capacity.

Everyone who entered the workhouses had to work. The men were engaged in grinding corn, breaking stones, or working the land. The women were engaged in house duties, washing, child minding, sewing, etc and there was no pay for the work done.

To qualify for relief, the whole family had to enter the workhouse together. On entry, families were segregated; fathers and sons into the male wards, mothers and daughters into the female wards and children into the children's wards. This gave rise to great worry and suffering as many families never saw each other again and were not aware of how other members of the family were faring.

In 1848, there were approximately 130,000 inmates in workhouses - 190,000 in 1849, 210,000 in 1850 and a peak of 217,000 in 1851. Overcrowding was a common problem, fever and disease was rampant and death rates were high. There were, for example, 502 inmates in the workhouse in Clifden, Co Galway on 14 October 1848, although officially it could only accommodate 302 people.

Workhouse Diets

ADULTS *(Male and female over 15 years)*

Breakfast	8 oz oatmeal made into "stirabout" and one pint of mixed milk
Dinner	3½ lb potatoes and 1 pint buttermilk
Meal times	*Breakfast 9.30 am; Dinner 4.30 pm*

CHILDREN *(Over 2 years)*

Breakfast	4 oz oatmeal made into stirabout and ½ pint milk
Dinner	2 lb potatoes, ½ pint buttermilk
Supper	4 oz bread, ½ pint buttermilk
Meal times	*Breakfast 9.00 am; Dinner 2.00 pm and Supper 7.00 pm*

When potatoes were unavailable during the Famine, the diet was changed. From 1847 the "established diet" was as follows:

ADULTS

Breakfast	2 oz rice, 6 oz Indian meal, 1 pint buttermilk
Dinner	10 oz Indian meal, 1 pint buttermilk

CHILDREN *(9-15 years)*

Breakfast	1½ oz rice, 4.5 oz Indian meal, ⅓ quart buttermilk
Dinner	6 oz Indian meal, quart buttermilk
Supper	¼ lb bread, 1 naggin sweetmilk

Source : The Past, Ui Cinsealaigh Historical Society, 1972

The Workhouse at Clifden, Co. Galway.

Interior view of a women's dormitory probabley in an English Workhouse

Children's sleeping platforms, Birr workhouse, Co Offaly. The children slept on straw on the platforms.

The diets introduced during the Famine were much lower in energy and vitamin C than the pre-Famine diets as can be seen from the figures in Table 7.

Table 7 : Percentage of recommended daily nutrient requirements supplied by the Enniscorthy workhouse diets before and during the Famine.

	Energy %	*Protein %*	*Vitamin C %*
Potato diet (pre-Famine)*			
Adult males	93	139	442
Adult females	120	177	442
Children (over 2 years)	87	136	342
*Workhouse diet ** (during Famine)*			
Adult males	33	77	49
Adult females	42	98	49
Children (over 2 years)	46	95	70

** Potatoes, oatmeal, buttermilk*

*** Rice, Indian meal, buttermilk*

Chapter 7

Consequences of the Famine

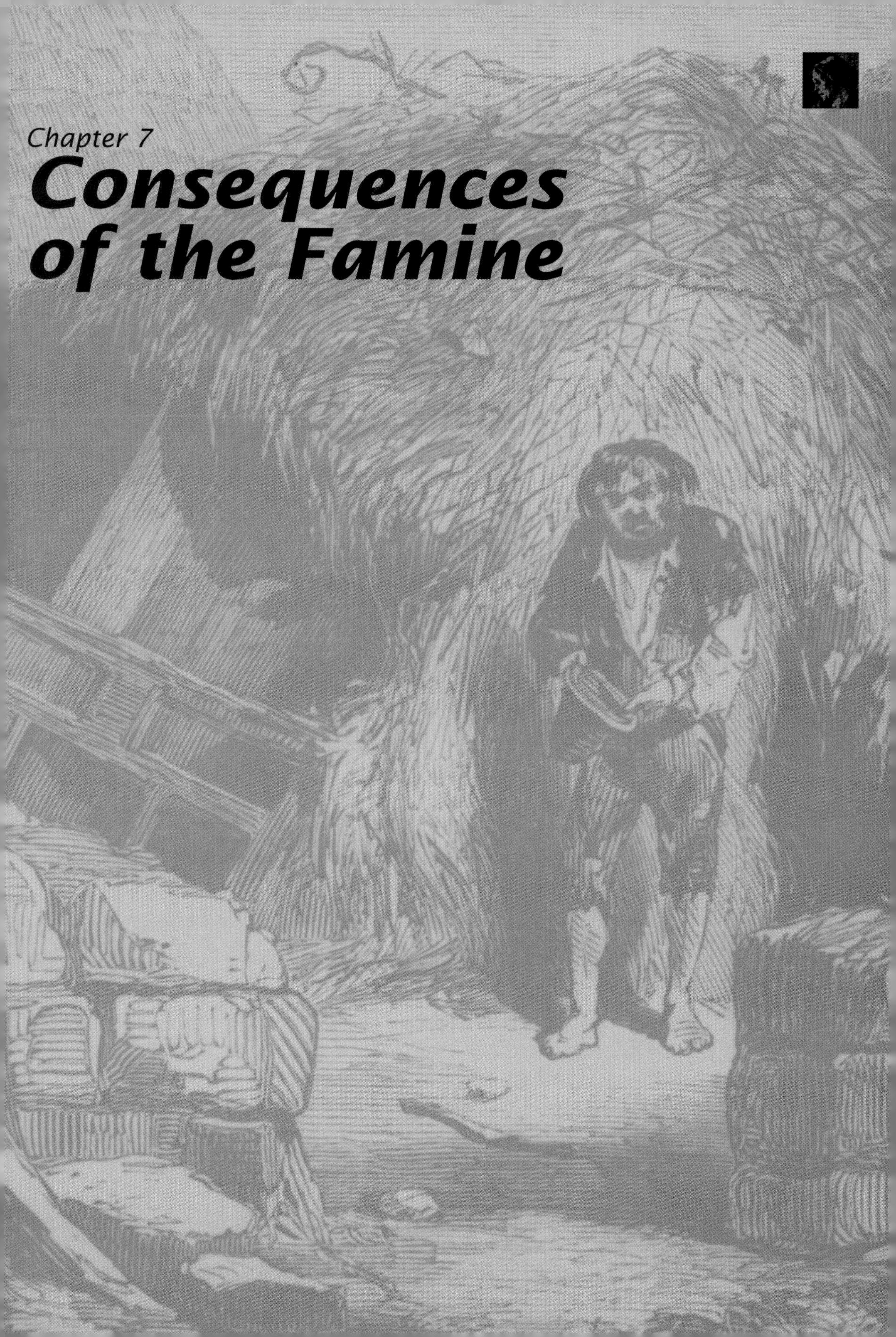

Consequences of the Famine.

Disease.

The main diseases which became epidemic during the Famine included:

Typhus

The disease was transmitted by lice and was known as "Black Fever". The death rate was high.

Relapsing Fever

Recurring fever, transmitted by lice.

Dysentery

Diarrhoea,not usually fatal except to children, caused by the sparsity of diet and liquid diets.

Bacillary Dysentery

Transmitted by infected persons handling food supplies. It caused death in many cases.

Hunger Oedema

Swelling of the limbs and then the body until the body finally burst.

Scurvy

Also called "Black Leg". It caused joints to become enlarged, teeth to fall out and the blood vessels under the skin to burst. Caused by lack of vitamin C in the diet.

Ophthalmia

Affected the eyes, especially of children, causing blindness, generally in one eye. Over 13,000 cases were recorded in 1849 and 27,000 cases in 1850. Caused by a lack of vitamin A in the diet.

Asiatic Cholera

Was epidemic between January and May 1849.

Fever

- Once fever was brought into an area it became epidemic and raged for months.
- The Fever Bill (April 1847) by putting medical facilities in place, ensuring the burial of bodies and hygiene helped to control the epidemic.
- It is probable that of the one million or more people who died during the Famine, in 85 - 90% of cases death was attributed to fever/disease rather than starvation.

Evictions.

The Famine led to growing arrears in rent and rates among small farmers. This, allied to the Poor Law which made landlords liable for the rates of tenants paying under £4 in rent, led to a wave of evictions during the Famine.

Evictions.

1846	4,000 families
1847	6,000 families
1848	9,500 families
1849	16,500 families
1850	20,000 families
1851	13,000 families

Sources: Daly and Litton

Evicted families could not be given shelter by relatives or friends and had to seek shelter in ditches, scalps and bog holes.

The village of Moveen near Kilkee, Co. Clare, cleared during the Famine

There were also thousands of "voluntary surrenders" by people who could not pay and accepted some settlement, subsidised emigration or a promise of a workhouse place.

The scene at a Famine eviction in Co. Tipperary was described by Sir William Butler in later years.

> *"One day I was taken to the scene of an eviction... where some dozen houses were to be pulled down and the people evicted... the sheriff, a strong body of police and the crowbar brigade... were present.*
>
> *At a signal from the sheriff the work began. The miserable inmates were dragged out, the thatched roofs were torn down and the earthen walls battered in by crowbars; the screaming women, the half naked children, the paralysed grandmother and the tottering grandfather were hauled out..."*

The evicted families could not be given shelter by relatives or friends or they too might be evicted. Instead they would shelter in ditches or bog holes, try to enter the workhouse or wander the roads until they succumbed to disease and death.

Emigration

The second failure of the potato crop in 1846 totally changed the attitude of the Irish peasant to emigration. People who had previously regarded "emigration as the most terrible of all fates" now wanted to get out of Ireland.

Emigration to America and Canada

1846	116,000
1847	230,000
1848-50	200,000 annually
1851	225,000
1852-54	195,000 annually

- Over 2 million people (25% of the population) left Ireland in the decade 1845 to 1855. No other population movement of the 19th century was on so great a scale.
- Entire familes went.
- Irish Famine emigrants had a major influence on the developement of other countries. At the time the population of the USA, Canada and Britain was about 23 milllion, 1 million and 14 million people, respectively. An idea of the impact of the population movement can be gauged when it is considered that 37,000 Irish emigrants joined the 115,000 citizens of Boston in 1847.

The priest blessing Irish emigrants as they prepare to leave home.

Who went?

The first to go in 1846 were the prosperous. When they arrived in Quebec, they were described as "well to do, healthy and with a little capital". Soon however, the poor, fleeing famine and starvation arrived and the authorities in the United States and Canada complained bitterly about being "made the poor house of Europe".

- The poor who could raise fares were leaving.
- With the total cost of the Famine transferred to the rates, tenant farmers, frustrated at the hopeless struggle to make ends meet, were also leaving.

"Let me go to the land of liberty
let me see no more of the
titheman and the taxman"

Source: Miller and Wagner, 1994.

A letter from Mary Rush to her parents in Canada who had emigrated earlier is an example of the appeals sent to relations for money or passage tickets.

6th September 1846.

Dear Father and Mother,

Pen cannot describe the poverty of this country at present. The potato crop is quite done away all over Ireland. There is nothing expected here, only an immediate famine. If you don't endeavour to take us out of it, it will be the first news you will hear by some friend of me and my little family lost by hunger.

Michael and Mary.

Source: Miller and Wagner, 1994.

Thousands of Irish responded to such appeals and thousands of emigrants in 1846/'47 saved to send passage money to family members left behind in Ireland. The system of chain emigration then initiated continued up to the 1960s.

The "Coffin Ships" of 1847.

Even healthy people found the journey to America and Canada arduous. Those weakened by famine found it a nightmare. By the Autumn of 1846, the authorities in America and Canada were complaining that destitute Irish were arriving. The USA soon introduced regulations to make it dearer and more difficult to enter that country. Thus, the poor had no choice but to set out for Canada hoping to enter the USA overland.

Despite medical inspections many sick people were allowed aboard ships in 1847 spreading fever and disease.

- Approximately 100,000 emigrants set out for Canada in 1847.
- Fares were cheaper than those to America because the regulations were less strict and the ships involved were primarily engaged in bringing timber to Britain.

- Mortality rates of from 20% to 40% on board ship were common. Fever, shortages of water and food, overcrowding and unhygienc conditions were all contributory factors.
- Once landed the quarantine facilities were unable to cope with the flood of sick immigrants. It is estimated that at least 5,300 immigrants died at "Grosse Isle" and a further 6,000 at "Point St. Charles" in 1847.
- Fever followed the immigrants to Montreal and Quebec where, because of the dread of sickness, most found it difficult to get work.
- After 1847 stricter controls were enforced and death rates during emigration fell dramatically.

Immigrant Life

Famine immigrants to the United States and Canada had to accept poor jobs, low wages and appalling living conditions. Most had to start life anew at the bottom of the socio - economic ladder. For many years, being Irish and particularly Irish and Catholic was a stigma in American society. Gradually, however, the Irish in the United States became established and prominent in business, labour, political, religious and cultural life.

Women accounted for half of all post-Famine Irish emigrants

Of the many nationalities of immigrants to the United States, post-Famine Irish emigrants were unique in two respects:

(1) As many women as men emigrated The majority were single unattached women who emigrated to avail of better job and marriage prospects.
(2) Very few returned to live in Ireland.

Emigration to Britain.

Many of the poorest of the Famine emigrants went to Britain. There they spread around the country but many never escaped destitution. It is estimated that about 20% of the six to seven million people who emigrated since the Famine have gone to Britain.

Population Decline.

The population of almost all countries increased substantially in the late nineteenth and early twentieth century. In Ireland, however, the population declined by almost half between 1845 and 1911. Anong the main reasons were:

- Rising age at marriage - for males marriage age increased from 23 to 33 years and for females from 22 to 28 years.
- Declining marriage rate - the proportion of males aged 45 to 54 years and never married rose from 10.2% in 1841 to 27.3% in 1911. For females, the corresponding figures were 12.5% to 24.9%, respectively.
- Changing rural structure - end of sub-division of farms and gradual consolidation.
- Emigration - the outflow of about 5 million people between 1845 and 1911 was enormous.
- Declining birth rate - births per 1,000 of population fell from 35 before the Famine to 28 by 1870 and 25 by 1914.

Figure 13: The percentage population decline by county between 1841 and 1851.

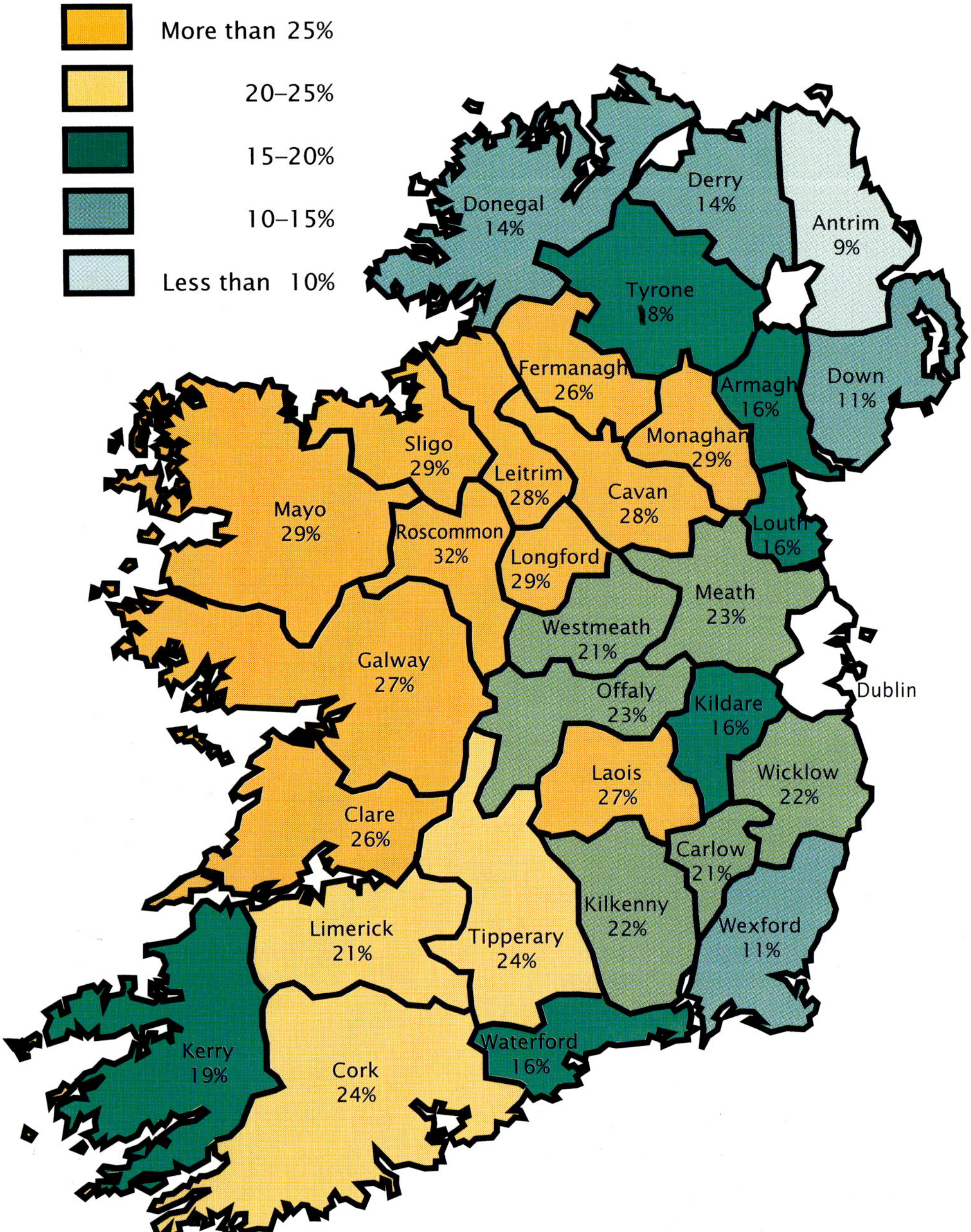

(Courtesy of Mayo County Libary.)

Farm Size

Table 8: Post-Famine change in the number and size of farm holdings.

Size of Holding	*1845*	*1847*	*1851*	*1910*
1 to 5 acres	182,000	140,000	88,000	62,000
5 to 15 acres	311,000	270,000	192,000	154,000
Over 15 acres	277,000	321,000	290,000	304,000
Total	770,000	730,000	570,000	520,000

After Bourke and Lee

As can be seen from the figures in Table 8, the number of small holdings declined substantially during the Famine. It can also be noted that trends set during the Famine continued over the following 60 years, but at a slower rate. However, as a country Ireland remained rural in nature throughout the nineteenth century. There were still 520,000 farm holdings in 1910. The number of farms has since declined to less than 170,000 of which in 1991, 90,000 were of less than 20 hectares (50 acres) in size.

Post-Famine Recovery

The process of recovery after the famine brought change for all social classes. For landlords, their position was never as secure again. Lost income from rents and high rates led to bankruptcy for 10% of landlords. The Encumbered Estates Act (1849) made it easier for purchasers to acquire estates in debt. Within ten years, about one seventh of the country and within a generation, about a quarter of the country changed hands.

For tenants, the Famine brought an opportunity to increase the size of their holding. Political awareness also developed with tenants demanding recognition as legitimate owners of the land. Fair rent, fixity of tenure and free sale were demanded.

The Land Act of 1880 introduced by Gladstone set up land courts to arbitrate on fair rents in given circumstances. The Act also guaranteed fixity of tenure to the tenant provided the rent was paid, and gave the tenant a right to compensation for improvements made.

The co-operative movement was founded in the late 1880's.

Within a few years, further Land Acts facilitated the sale of estates to tenants on the payment of an annuity.

Developments which consolidated the process of change were the formation of the co-operative movement in the late 1880's, the Irish Agricultural Organising Society in 1894 and the Department of Agriculture and Technical Instruction in 1899.

Housing and diet both improved. The number of one roomed houses declining until there were less than 4,000 in 1911. Outhouses for animals became more common and the practice among poor families of keeping animals in the living room declined rapidly.

Emigration continued as in most parts of the county land was no longer sub-divided.This left all children, exept the inheritor, to find employment or to emigrate.

Women were the backbone of the rural farming communities, running the household, raising children and usually rearing pigs, chickens and sometimes goats. Carding, dying and spinning wool were also considered to be female tasks. They were also involved in harvesting crops, cutting and carrying home the turf and there was no taboo against women undertaking hard physical labour.

In managing all these activities - selling butter, vegetables, eggs and poultry - women controlled a large proportion of the family budget.

Grain, potatoes and livestock each accounted for about one third of the value of agricultural output in 1845. After the Famine, grain output decreased while the livestock sector developed.

The number of cattle and sheep almost doubled in the 50 years after the Famine. Poultry also increased from 10 million to 27 million.

For over 20 years agriculture prospered until the late 1870's when there was a major recession as both crop yields and prices fell. Soon, many small holders had difficulty in paying the rents and evictions followed.

Even after the Famine, agriculture in the west remained weak. A report at the time stated that there were two classes in the west, the poor and the destitute.

In an attempt to improve conditions in these heavily populated areas, the Congested Districts Board was formed in 1891. Cash was injected into the area to raise living standards and to provide employment.

Road building schemes were introduced and development of the fishing industry was encouraged.

Often small children were expected to make an economic contribution to family income and were regularly sent to work in factories. An eight year old was allowed to work 10 hours a day, three days a week, while attending school for two and a half days. A 12 year old could be employed full time.

Women were involved in the hard physical farm work.

In an attempt to improve living conditions in the heavily populated western areas, The Congested Districts Board was formed in 1891.

In rural towns, hiring fairs were held regularly and children from as young as 10 years were hired out for keep and small wages for periods of six months. For poor families, this meant the children were no longer a drain on scarce resources.

Transport

The expansion of the railway network immediately after the Famine played a major part in opening up the country to trade and rapid information movement. There were 2,000 miles of track by 1870 and 3,500 miles by 1914.

The popularity of the bicycle, and the increase in the number of horses and traps, dray carts, etc all helped to increase the mobility of rural populations, ease manual work loads and improve trade and enterprise. This in turn led to an increase in the population of towns and cities, which jumped from about 15% of the population at the time of the Famine to 35% at the turn of the century.

The change from tillage-based agriculture to livestock enterprises and the very slow progress of industry meant that rural towns developed very slowly after the Famine. The growth of imports which included clothing and footwear also contributed to this slow development.

However, the rise in general living standards as the century progressed brought increased purchasing power, more trading, improved overall prosperity and an upturn in the fortunes of towns.

Chapter 8

The Search for a Cure

The Search for a Cure

The Famine stimulated great interest among scientists and landowners in finding a cure for blight. The search was to take almost 40 years and it started on a controversial note.

One group of scientists were of the opinion that "the failure of the potato was caused by a fungus". Another group were of the opinion that "the failure was caused by the cheerless weather". Soon the scientists who attributed the cause to the weather gained the upper hand. This was largely because in the 1840s the accepted wisdom was that spores, bacteria, and germs were not a cause but a consequence of disease.

Irish Interest.

The first written observation of blight in Ireland was made by Dr. David Moore, Curator, Botanic Gardens, Dublin, on the 20th August 1845. He was soon satisfied that it was a fungus which attacked the potato plant.

Dr. David Moore

The basic life cycle of the blight fungus was eventually worked out by A. de Barry in 1865. He later named the fungus as Phytophthora (1876). The adjective infestans had already been put forward by Montague (France) almost 30 years earlier.

Prevention.

In 1882 a preventative chemical for potato blight was stumbled on by accident. Monsieur Millardet (France) noticed that grapes in a vineyard bordering the road which had been sprayed with a mixture of copper sulphate and hydrated lime to prevent thefts, had remained free from downy mildew, a fungus related to Phytophthora infestans (blight). By 1885 M. Millardet had demonstrated the effectiveness of this spray treatment for the control of blight.

Progress in Ireland

The potato crop in Ireland was again severely affected by blight in 1870. As a result, a Select Committee was appointed by the House of Commons to make recommendations.

At the time it was believed that the only way to combat blight was to breed varieties resistant to the disease. In 1881, Professor Thomas Carroll was appointed Superintendent of the Albert Institution, Glasnevin, Dublin, under the National Board of Education to implement the recommendations of the Select Committee Report. He was a strong advocate of breeding for blight resistance and set about the task enthusiastically. By 1890 however, he had concluded that "none of these new varieties appear to equal the Champion", a variety introduced in 1876 and he decided to replicate the spraying experiments conducted in France.

Early equipment for the mixing and application of blight sprays.

Professor Carroll finalised instructions on the preparation of the Bordeaux Mixture, times of application, thoroughness of dressing and weather conditions at time of spraying in 1892. These instuctions were first issued in 1893.

Early publicity to promote spraying for blight control.

Dr. Austin Bourke.

Soon the promotion of spraying, the distribution of knapsack sprayers and the appointment of Agricultural Instructors helped to ensure that spraying for blight became routine practice in the cultivation of potatoes in Ireland.

The weather influences the development and spread of the disease and forecasting systems for potato blight are in place in many countries. Dr. Ausin Bourke of the Irish Meteorlogical Service played a major role in developing blight forecasting so as to better advise potato growers on the timing of blight sprays.

The first field station for the scientific investigation of blight and other diseases of potatoes was set up in Cliften, Co. Galway in 1909 by the Department of Agriculture and Technical Institution the forerunner of the present day Department of Agriculture, Food and Forestry.

Potato Blight Today

Blight is still the most important disease affecting the potato crop in Ireland. Despite improvements in varieties, fungicides, spraying equipment and disease forecasting, control is still far from perfect. The reason for this is that the fungus which causes blight (Phytophthora infestans) has shown amazing genetic diversity and variation. Strains have developed fungicide resistance, show variation in aggressiveness and recently the existence of a second mating type has been confirmed.

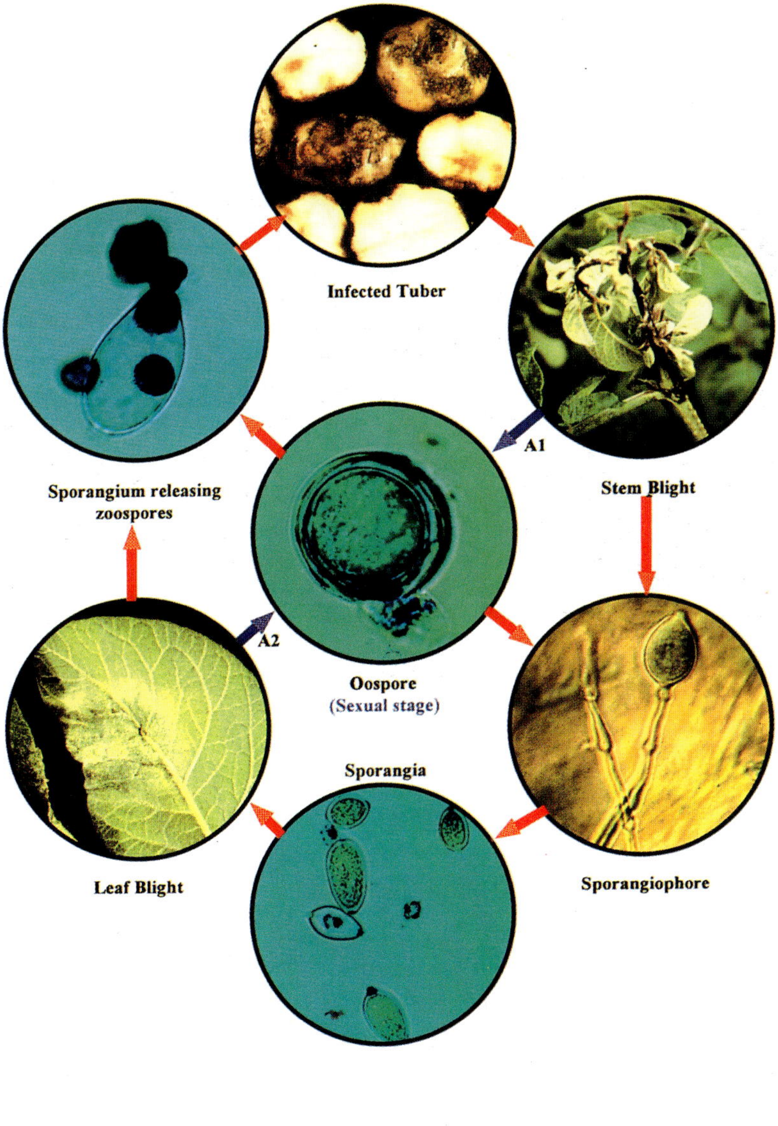

The disease cycle of Phytophthora infestans, the potato blight fungus.

Harvesting Early Potatoes in Co. Waterford in 1908

Advances in blight control

- Burgundy mixture (copper sulphate and washing soda) and Bordeaux mixture (copper sulphate and hydrated lime) - use persisted into the 1950's.
- Dithiocarbamates introduced in 1934.

Both of the above protect the potato plant from the fungus but need to be applied before the blight appears and need frequent reapplication.

- Organotins introduced in the 1960's. These products are protectants and also give greater tuber resistance to blight.
- Systemic fungicides introduced in the 1970's. These allow a greater interval between spraying and give protection to new growth.
- Translaminar fungicides introduced in the 1980's. These are partly systemic in action.

The testing and monitoring of fungicides for blight control is undertaken by Teagasc at the Oak Park Research Centre, Carlow.

The Potato Today

Today, Ireland still has the highest per capita consumption of potatoes in the European Union at 139 kg per person per year. Corresponding consumption figures for the UK and Portugal are 105 kg per person, Spain 103 kg, Belgium and Luxembourg 91 kg. Consumption is lower in Greece (84 kg), Holland (83 kg), Germany (73 kg), France (70 kg) and Denmark (57 kg). The least amount are consumed in Italy at just 12 kg per person per year.

Flouriness

People eating potatoes describe them as "floury" or "soapy". The flouriness of potatoes is related to the dry matter content and density of the potato.

- Floury potatoes - tubers of over 20% dry matter, eg Golden Wonder, Kerrs Pink, Record.
- Soapy potatoes - tubers under 18% dry matter, eg Cara, King Edward and the early potatoes from Cyprus, Italy etc.

About 60% of Irish consumers have a strong preference for high dry matter or "floury" potatoes.

Flouriness of potatoes is related to dry matter content. On left a "floury" potato variety and on the right a "soapy" variety.

Lessons from the Famine Experience

The Cross marking the Famine Pits at Bantry Cemetery. The caption on the base reads, "To mark the Famine Pits of 1846-8. May God give rest to the souls of the faithful departed."

Famines still happen in parts of the world, though thankfully no longer in Ireland. As a nation, Irish people are generally conscious of the hardship and suffering endured by our ancestors and respond with symnpathy for the victims of similar tragedies. Stimulating our response to present day catastrophies are the lessons learnt from the Irish Famine experience.

- It is estimated that a 10% shortfall in food supplies can give rise to famine as the more able hoard and scramble to protect supplies.
- Food supplies in Ireland were reduced by at least 10% in 1845 and by some 25-30% in 1846, 1847 and 1848.
- The poor cannot afford to pay famine prices for food supplies and the surest way to prevent deaths and distress is through food aid.
- Public sympathy and subscriptions reduce over time as famine fatigue, impatience and irritation with the problem develop.
- The Government of a famine affected area must be actively involved in providing and stimulating relief efforts. Attention must also be devoted to health care to prevent/curtail disease epidemics.
- Public works are an expensive, and not necessarily an effective method of dealing with famine.
- Government decisions should not exasperate the problem. Some decisions taken during the Irish famine had major negative consequences.

Reconstruction of a Famine house showing the clothes and cooking utensils typical of the period.

Quarter Acre Clause; any family who gave up their small-holding to get temporary relief had no home to return to or a means of making a living
Poor Law Extension Bill; because landlords were liable for the rates on small holdings, they evicted tenants who could not pay
Encumbered Estates Act; allowed forced sale of holdings with debts. The purchasers evicted tenants in many cases

Bibliography

This book sets out to be a concise outline of the Famine. As a consequence, a lot of detail has been omitted. The list of books consulted in researching this topic refer readers to a varied selection of detailed works ranging from the scholarly to photographic reminders of times past.

Bell, Jonathan	PEOPLE AND THE LAND, Belfast, 1992
Bradley, Ann Kathleen	THE HISTORY OF THE IRISH IN AMERICA, London
Bourke, Austin	THE VISITATION OF GOD? Dublin, 1993
Campbell, Stephen J.	THE GREAT IRISH FAMINE, Co Roscommon, 1994
Cappamore His. Soc.	CAPPAMORE: A PARISH HISTORY, 1992
Carty, James	IRELAND FROM GRATTANS PARLIAMENT TO THE GREAT FAMINE, Dublin, 1949
Daly, Mary E.	THE FAMINE IN IRELAND, Dundalk, 1986
Davidson, W D	THE HISTORY OF THE POTATO IN IRELAND, Department of Agriculture, Dublin. 34:286-307, 1937
Dowley, Leslie J	THE FAILURE OF THE POTATO CROP 1845-48, Teagasc, Carlow, 1995
Edwards & Williams	THE GREAT FAMINE - STUDIES IN IRISH HISTORY 1845 -52, Dublin,1994
Evans, E. Estyn	IRISH FOLK WAYS, London, 1957
Evans, E. Estyn	THE PERSONALITY OF IRELAND, Belfast 1981
Galway Roots	JOURNAL OF THE GALWAY FAMILY HISTORY SOCIETY, Vol 3, 1995
Kee, Robert	IRELAND A HISTORY, London, 1982
Kinealy, Christine	THIS GREAT CALAMITY, Dublin, 1994
Lee, Joseph	THE MODERNISATION OF IRISH SOCIETY 1848-1918, Dublin 1973
Litton, Helen	THE IRISH FAMINE - AN ILLUSTRATED HISTORY, Dublin 1994
Miller & Wagner	OUT OF IRELAND, London, 1994
O'Connell, Michael	SHADOWS - AN ALBUM OF THE IRISH PEOPLE 1841-1914, Dublin, 1985
O'Connor, John	THE WORKHOUSES OF IRELAND, Dublin, 1995
O Grada, Cormac	IRELAND BEFORE AND AFTER THE FAMINE, Manchester, 1988
O Grada, Cormac	IRELAND A NEW ECONOMIC HISTORY 1780-1939, Oxford, 1994
Rees, Jim	A FAREWELL TO FAMINE, Arklow, 1994
Salaman, R	THE HISTORY AND SOCIAL INFLUENCE OF THE POTATO, Cambridge University Press, 1949
Schofield, C; Sexton, S	IRELAND - PHOTOGRAPHS 1840-1930, London, 1994
Somerville, Alexander	LETTERS FROM IRELAND DURING THE FAMINE, Dublin, 1994
Thomson, D and McGusty,	Irish Journals of Elizabeth Smith, Oxford, 1980
Walker, Brian M.	FACES OF IRELAND, Belfast, 1992
O'Broin Art; McMahon, Sean	
Woodham-Smith, Cecil	THE GREAT HUNGER OF IRELAND 1845-1849, London, 1991

ist of illustrations

Cover

Illustrated London News (ILN) courtesy of the National Library of Ireland (NLI)

Chapter 1

5 Illustrated London News, NLI
7 **A Kerry Bride and Bridegroom**, from Hall's Ireland, its scenery and character; London, 1841-3
11 **Class 4** and **Class 2 Houses**, Illustrated London News; Class 3 and Class 1 houses drawn from Laurence Collection photographs, NLI
13 **Reconstructed famine cabin**, Teagasc
17 **The ejectment**, ILN
18 **Itinerant labourers**, watercolour by Samuel Towgood Roche, by courtesy Ulster Folk and Transport Museum
20 **Cabin interior**, The Pictorial Times, Feb 1846; courtesy of National Library of Scotland
20 **The house of Pat Brennan**, The Pictorial Times, Feb 1846, courtesy of National Library of Scotland
22 **Emigrants on deck**, ILN, courtesy NLI

Chapter 2

23 **Idealised pre-famine scene**, watercolour by Aislinn Adams for Teagasc
24 Sir Walter Raleigh
26/27 **Pre-famine potato varieties**, photographs by Charles Godson, Teagasc
29 **The potato murrin**, ILN 1846, courtesy NLI
31/32 **Potato blight**, photographs courtesy Leslie Dowley, Teagasc

Chapter 4

35 **Alexis Soyer's model soup kitchen in Dublin**, ILN, April 1847; courtesy NLI
36 **Sir Robert Peel**, ILN 1846, courtesy NLI
37 **Anti corn law petition**, ILN 1846; courtesy NLI
38 **Deciding Ireland's fate**. Top left and right, Hulton Deutsch Collection; Lower left, ILN courtesy NLI
39 **Failure of the potato crop**. The Pictorial Times, Aug 1846; courtesy National Library of Scotland
42 **Famine relief wall**, courtesy Tom Maher, Teagasc
43 **Famine soup boiler**, Teagasc
44 **Cork Society of Friends, soup kitchen**, ILN, Jan 1847; courtesy NLI

Chapter 5

45 **Searching for potatoes in West Cork**, ILN, Feb 1847, courtesy NLI
46 **Mother at Clonakilty**, Co Cork, ILN, Feb. 1849, courtesy NLI
47 **The Mullins hut at Schull**. (Seated the Rev Robert Trail who died of Famine Fever some months later), ILN, Feb. 1847, courtesy NLI
48 **Famine funeral**, ILN, Feb. 1847, courtesy NLI
49 **Digging for potatoes**, ILN, Dec 1849; courtesy NLI
49 **Seeking admission to the workhouse**, Robert Wilson, The Life and Times of Queen Victoria, 1887-88

50 **A victim of the Famine**, Drawing by A MacLure from Narrative of a Journey from Oxford to Skibbereen, 1847
51 **Dungarvan**, ILN 1847, courtesy NLI
52 **Driving cattle**, ILN, Dec 1849, courtesy NLI

Chapter 6

55/56 **Captain Kennedy**, Kilrush, distributing clothes to the evicted, ILN, Dec 1849; courtesy NLI
59 **Typical workhouse**, Illustration courtesy of The Irish Architectural Archive, Dublin
60 **The Workhouse at Clifden**, ILN, Jan 1850; courtesy NLI
61 **Workhouse Interior**, courtesy Gill and MacMillan
61 **Children's Dormitory**, Birr Workhouse, courtesy P Cotter photography

Chapter 7

63 **Evicted tenant within his tumbled house**, ILN, 15 Dec 1849, courtesy NLI
65 **Day after the ejectment** (left) ILN, Dec 1845; courtesy NLI, on right also ILN
66 **Village of Moveen**, ILN, Dec 1849, courtesy NLI
67 **Irish emigrants set out for America**, ILN, May 1851; courtesy NLI
69 **Government Inspectors Office**, ILN, courtesy NLI
70 **Women emigrants**, Laurence Collection, courtesy NLI
74/75/76 Photographs courtesy NLI

Chapter 8

78 **Dr David Moore**, engraved portrait courtesy National Botanic Gardens, Dublin
79 **Early spraying equipment for blight**, assembled by Martin Kelly, Co Kildare
79 **Effectiveness of spraying**, courtesy Department of Agriculture, Food and Forestry, Dublin
80 **Dr. Austin Bourke**, photograph courtesy Department of Agriculture, Food and Forestry, Dublin
80 **Pethybridge Laboratory**, photograph courtesy Department of Agriculture, Food and Forestry, Dublin
81 **Phytophthora infestans**, Teagasc
82 **Early Potatoes**, courtesy Department of Agriculture, Food and Forestry, Dublin
83 **Floury and Soapy Potatoes**, courtesy Harry Kehoe, Teagasc

84 **Bantry Cemetery**, Teagasc
85 **Famine Exhibition**, Teagasc

About the author

John Keating M.Agr.Sc. is a native of Co. Tipperary. He has worked in information and public relations with the Department of Agriculture, Food and Forestry, ACOT and is currently with Teagasc – The Agriculture and Food Development Authority. Presently he is editor of the bi-monthly publication *'Today's Farm'* and Head of Information and PR at Teagasc.